Generation Y
for ROOKIES

Titles in the *for* ROOKIES series

About the author

Sally Bibb is an expert in Generation Y, trust and employee engagement. She is co-founder of talentsmoothie, a specialist Generation Y consultancy, and founder of Engaging Minds, a communications and engagement consultancy.

During her career Sally has worked in international organizational change roles in the telecoms and media sectors. Before setting up her own consultancies Sally was a director at The Economist Group. Her first degree was in Psychology, Sociology and Economics, and she has an MSc in Organizational Change from the University of Surrey.

Sally frequently speaks at conferences, seminars and dinner engagements. She is also a writer, editor and award-winning author of several books and many articles on the subject of trust and organizational change.

You can read Sally's blog at www.talentsmoothie.com/blog/ or contact her at sallybibb@talentsmoothie.com

Generation Y
for ROOKIES

First published in 2010 by Marshall Cavendish Business
An imprint of Marshall Cavendish International
PO Box 65829
London EC1P 1NY
United Kingdom
info@marshallcavendish.co.uk
and
1 New Industrial Road
Singapore 536196
genrefsales@sg.marshallcavendish.com
www.marshallcavendish.com/genref

A member of **BPR**

businesspublishersroundtable.com

Marshall Cavendish is a trademark of Times Publishing Limited

Other Marshall Cavendish offices: Marshall Cavendish International (Asia) Private
Limited, 1 New Industrial Road, Singapore 536196 • Marshall Cavendish Corporation.
99 White Plains Road, Tarrytown NY 10591–9001, USA • Marshall Cavendish International
(Thailand) Co Ltd. 253 Asoke, 12th Floor, Sukhumvit 21 Road, Klongtoey Nua, Wattana,
Bangkok 10110, Thailand • Marshall Cavendish (Malaysia) Sdn Bhd, Times Subang, Lot 46,
Subang Hi-Tech Industrial Park, Batu Tiga, 40000 Shah Alam, Selangor Darul Ehsan,
Malaysia

The authors and publisher have used their best efforts in preparing this book and disclaim
liability arising directly and indirectly from the use and application of this book.

All reasonable efforts have been made to obtain necessary copyright permissions. Any
omissions or errors are unintentional and will, if brought to the attention of the publisher,
be corrected in future printings.

A CIP record for this book is available from the British Library

ISBN 978-0-462-09980-4

Illustrations by Nuria Aparicio and Joan Guardiet

Printed and bound in Singapore by Fabulous Printers Pte Ltd

Contents

Author's note

Generation Y is also variously known as "Gen Y", "the Net Gen", "Millennials" and "Y-ers". For the sake of consistency, in this book I generally use the term Gen Y.

I generally refer to Baby Boomers as Boomers, and Generation X as Gen X.

Introduction

There is so much being written and discussed today on the subject of Generation Y – those people born between 1980 and 2000 (in other words, those under 30 at the time of writing). The discussion usually centres on how different they are from the other generations, and often features exasperation by those doing the commenting. There appear to be two distinct views of Generation (or Gen) Y. One is that their expectations are too high, they are far too demanding and impatient, and they need to change their attitudes if they are to fit into the world of work. The other is that they are a talented, interested and energetic group of people who will be key to helping organizations change and innovate in the years ahead.

Whatever your own view, Gen Y is a group of people that is important for organizations today. Because of global demographic changes, young talent is going to get scarcer and scarcer. At the time of writing, some of the big professional services companies' workforces are 40–50 per cent made up of under 30s, and currently 20 per cent of the UK workforce is drawn from Gen Y. When half your workforce has different values, attitudes and motivations from the other half, it's a good idea to understand them. If you don't, you could end up struggling to

2 get and keep the talent you need to run your business now and in the future.

Many organizations are becoming concerned about their ability to attract, retain and motivate Gen Y. I will stress at this point that I am not advocating pandering to or changing the workplace just for the sake of these under-30s. What I am suggesting is that a working environment that works equally well for all generations is a good thing. If you can motivate all of your employees, irrespective of their age, then they are likely to be more engaged and therefore more effective and productive.

Gen Y is certainly challenging prevailing organizational cultures, ways of managing and people practices. Some would say that the changes Gen Y is demanding are long overdue. I would certainly argue that much of what Gen Y wants from work, Baby Boomers (those born between 1946 and 1964) and Generation X (those born between 1965 and 1979) would have quite liked too, but unlike Gen Y they were conditioned not to expect it. Some see Gen Y as a problem, or at least a challenge. Others see them as an opportunity. Whatever your viewpoint, ignore Gen Y's changing needs at your peril.

This book is written for those who are interested in understanding more about Generation Y: managers, teachers, parents, and anyone else who is interested in finding out how to attract, motivate, manage and communicate with them – or just relate well to them. Usually (though not always) these people will be of an older generation – probably either Boomers or Gen X.

A word of caution at this point. I will be referring to the different generations' characteristics throughout this book and, for ease of explanation, generalizing about them. However, it is important to point out that it is of course impossible to generalize across an entire age group. I know some people aged 50+ who are more Gen Y in attitude than a couple of my twenty-something acquaintances. Generational mindset is more to do with attitude than age. The characteristics I describe will be true of most Gen Ys, but there will always be "outliers" – in other words, those who do not exhibit these characteristics. And there are differences between Gen Ys in different cultures.

The insight and knowledge contained in this book comes from two years of researching, studying and working with Gen Y and their older colleagues in organizations in the public, private and third sectors. I first became interested in Gen Y when I worked at The Economist Group (publisher of *The Economist* magazine). I noticed that the advertising and marketing sectors had identified this generation as being different from the rest of us. They had marked Gen Y out as a segment with a distinct psychographic profile, one that needed different kinds of messages and communications media.

I had also noticed that younger people who were joining The Economist Group were different from their older colleagues. Even compared with others in the challenging Economist Group culture, these young people were pushing beyond what their colleagues from other generations would tolerate.

Then in 2006 Maurice Saatchi, one half of the Saatchi brothers, major players in the advertising world, predicted the death of the 30-second television advert. He hypothesized that a number of different factors contributed to advertising being "cut down in its prime". These factors are sociological (families no longer sit together to watch television), technological (most households have a whole lot of technology and applications competing for attention, including computers, iPods, games and social computing technologies), and psychological. (The psychological factor relates to how the world is divided into "digital natives" and "digital immigrants", the young being digital natives: they learn technology like they learned their mother tongue. The rest of us – immigrants – will always have an "accent" and have to "translate".) Finally, Saatchi argued that the digital native's brain has come to be physically different as a result of the way it interacts with technology: "It has re-wired itself. It responds faster. It sifts out. It recalls less." This explains why young people are good at multitasking and can send instant messages while working on their laptops,

4 listening to music on their MP3s and watching TV, all at the same time. This multi-tasking results in a phenomenon called Continuous Partial Awareness (CPA). The upshot, said Saatchi, was that day-after recall scores for TV advertisements collapsed from 35 per cent in the 1960s to just 10 per cent in 1996.

The way that young people relate to media has clearly changed massively. This has far-reaching implications for anyone who is trying to sell to this consumer group. It clearly also has implications for those employing them. Back in 2006 I started to wonder why employers were not concerning themselves with Gen Y as a different and distinct category of worker. Given demographic changes and concerns about global talent shortages in particular, it seemed like a real oversight.

At that time I started to have a look at what was out there that could provide useful insight into Gen Y for employers. There were a number of books and some commentators, but it struck me that so much of what was being said was based on little or no evidence. I couldn't find a research base to back up claims that Gen Y was substantially different from the other generations, and therefore needed to be treated differently. Nor could I find any adequate explanation as to *why* they were different.

That was three years ago. This book is based upon the research that my business partners and I undertook into this area. It is also, and importantly, based on all the work we have done with over one hundred clients, many of them global, from all sectors. We have worked with them and helped them to understand and grapple with real and challenging problems. And we now understand the issues in a way that is possible only when you have immersed yourself in something and struggled with it for a good chunk of time. My network of clients, contacts and mentors from all generations have provided the opportunities to acquire knowledge, insight and wisdom that has enabled me to write this very practical book. It is based on solid insight and research, and its aim is to help you make the most of Gen Y as a very valuable resource.

By the time you finish this book you will understand Generation Y and how they differ from the other generations, but also, and most importantly, how to make the most of their unique strengths and ways of doing things.

6

Do you have Gen Y employees or children? If so, you will know that it can be very hard to understand them. They behave in ways that are sometimes strange and unfamiliar to the rest of us. They seem to prefer to communicate with their friends via instant messaging than by phone or face to face, they appear to get bored easily, they want instant gratification. Don't they? And the list goes on.

It's easy to get annoyed or frustrated by these young people and their strange ways. It is very easy to misunderstand them and why they do things the way they do.

CHAPTER 1

Understanding Generation Y (and why are they different from the other generations?)

What's the difference?

The following true story illustrates how different the generations are and how easy it is for conflict to arise between them. A young high-flier in an ad agency emailed the CEO to tell him that he disagreed with a decision that the CEO had taken. The CEO responded immediately, saying, "I have run this company for ten years and I think I know what I am doing." The young graduate replied, "I realize this is an uncomfortable conversation but I am not the only one who disagrees with this decision." He went on to give reasons and rationale as to why he disagreed. And the CEO, even though he had always said he welcomed feedback and had an "open-door" policy, was indignant at receiving this email from this young upstart.

I spoke to the graduate and asked him what he was thinking about when he sent the emails. He told me that he thought the company was great, that he cared about it, and that he didn't want to stay silent when he thought a mistake was being made. It did not occur to him that he might annoy his boss, and his boss's bosses, by going over their heads and emailing the CEO direct. He did not realize that the hierarchy and

8   your status within it was such a big deal. And he couldn't understand why he had received such a terse reply from the CEO. I had to explain to him that this fifty-something boss grew up in a very different time, when you didn't challenge the boss.

This was a clear case of the graduate not understanding the "rules of the game", and of each person judging the other on their behaviour, not on their intentions. What I mean by this is that we all observe other people's behaviour and make judgements based on that behaviour. Obviously we don't know what their thoughts, motives and intentions are, unless they share them with us. However we do know and understand our own intentions; even if sometimes someone misunderstands our behaviour, *we* know why we did what we did. In the story above, clearly the graduate knew exactly why he was sending the emails (and equally clearly his intentions were good). But the CEO was not privy to the graduate's intention; all he had to go on was his behaviour. He interpreted that behaviour as disrespectful, inappropriate and rude. And his own intention was also to protect the management line and organizational infrastructure that he perceived as important for the effective running of the company.

In the course of my work I have heard many stories like this. They are symptomatic of the difference in style between the generations. Each generation has knowledge and wisdom, and each can learn from the others. In order to make sure we create productive relationships that work, we need to get into the heads of Gen Y and really understand them.

This chapter will explain why Gen Y are as they are, and why they behave the way they do. It will give you an understanding of Generation Y that means you can attract, manage and motivate them in a way that benefits everyone.

Rookie Buster

Each generation has knowledge and wisdom, and each can learn from the others.

Who is Generation Y?

Gen Y are those born between 1980 and 2000.

For the first time ever, we have four generations in the workplace. As older people choose to stay on at work (through necessity or desire) we will experience the trials and tribulations of creating work environments that appeal to and make the most of all generations.

Here are the four workplace generations and their birth years:

Traditionalists	*Baby Boomers*	*Gen X*	*Gen Y*
Born pre 1945	Born 1946–1964	Born 1965–1979	Born 1980–2000

The conditions under which they grew up

If you are the manager or parent of a Gen Y you will have first-hand experience of how different from the rest of us they are.

Generational differences are accounted for by a combination of factors:

Age
Young people are always different from their elders because they have yet to develop into adults, and psychologically they are establishing their identity, so have a need to mark themselves out as different from their parents and elders.

The conditions that they grew up under
As Napoleon Bonaparte said, "If you want to know how a man thinks, imagine the world when they were young."

Some of the most powerful influencing factors in our lives are those that occur when we are in our formative years and becoming aware of the world around us.

Rookie Buster

"If you want to know how a man thinks, imagine the world when they were young."

The prevailing political, social and economic conditions when a person is in their teens and starting to become aware of the world are very influential in shaping who they are. For example, I was in my mid to late teens during the "Winter of Discontent". I remember Thatcherism and 3 million unemployed. Most of the men in my family (the women mostly didn't have jobs or careers) had had the same job for life.

The conscious and unconscious messages I received about work were that it was scarce, when you got a job you damn well hung on to it, you put up with filing and photocopying for the first year even though you had a good degree, and you certainly did not challenge authority.

Experiences

The experiences that young people have when they are growing up obviously have an impact on their values and how they see the world. For example, Gen Y grew up in a world where there have been a number of acts of global terrorism, on which politicians have focused as one of the key threats to our safety. They saw the collapse of the Twin Towers on 9/11, and the London, Bali and Mumbai bombings. Their world does not feel as safe as the world of a teenager in the 1960s and 1970s. They were promised no wars, and this promise has not been fulfilled. So they reject the aggressive approach to solving conflict. They prefer a collaborative approach to life and work, not a competitive one.

Rookie Buster

They prefer a collaborative approach to life and work, not a competitive one.

They have always experienced being able to connect with people (even those whom they don't know) around the world via the internet. This experience clearly influences their mindset, worldliness and attitude towards possibilities. They are the first generation to go on "gap years". Gen X-ers did rail trips around Europe if they were lucky. The world was a much bigger place back then!

What is Generation Y like?

There are many stereotypes and prejudices about Gen Y – both negative and positive. Here are some of the ones that I hear the most often.

The negatives

- They are slackers; they don't want to work hard.
- They are disrespectful of authority.
- They are impatient and want it all now.
- They have an over-inflated view of their own abilities.
- They are over-confident.
- They don't understand how important it is to follow company rules.
- They are too demanding and want constant attention.
- They are unrealistic about how far they can go.
- They expect too much management time.
- They don't understand corporate politics – they are naive.

12   The positives

- They are hungry and want to get on fast.
- They are creative and innovative and challenge the "rules".
- They are committed and hard-working.
- They will do what it takes to get on.
- They are confident and see no barriers.
- They are hungry for learning.
- They don't go after status for status's sake.
- They are flexible.
- They are optimistic.

Despite all the positives, most of what I hear about Generation Y are comments from managers who are at a loss to understand them and deal with them. They see them as a problem to be solved.

I have talked to many organizations who have wasted time and money (and damaged relationships) because they have made incorrect assumptions. One example was a financial services company who had decided to launch a volunteering programme for their graduates. Their assumption was that Gen Y cared about corporate social responsibility (CSR) and would want to be involved in CSR programmes. But the programme was a flop – very few people were enthusiastic about it (although they didn't have a choice about doing it, because it was mandatory), and the feedback the company received afterwards was not good. I advised them to talk to the graduates to dig down and find out why. The answer was very simple. Although they did think that CSR was important, they preferred to give money to charities they cared about rather get involved in a programme at work. In some ways their attitude was more similar to a Gen X attitude. The lesson was that the graduates who were attracted to this company were in fact dissimilar to

Gen Y in their attitude to CSR, but the company had made the assumption that they were the same.

The first step is therefore to understand them and why they are as they are, so that you don't make assumptions. That is half the battle. Once you understand them it becomes much easier to know how to work with them. And it becomes clear how they can contribute to and shape the changing world of work.

Let's take a look at Generation Y's world.

They have grown up in mainly good economic times. Even in an economic downturn they remain optimistic. They see fewer barriers than older generations do and are more flexible. So whilst their behaviour changes somewhat in an economic crisis, their attitudes and values don't. Some of my clients have suggested that when the going gets tough, Gen Y will just become like Gen X. They won't – and the reason why they won't is because of the conditioning that we explored earlier in this chapter.

Their relationships with others

Hierarchy vs social networks

The internet has given Gen Y the ability to connect and collaborate with people all over the world. They are used to being able to connect with whoever they want or need to. Their world is a social network, not a hierarchy. They see their Gen X and Boomer colleagues complaining about being in back-to-back meetings, talking about how unproductive these meetings are, and longing for time at their desk. To Gen Y, this is bizarre on two counts – the first is they can't understand why people don't just make sure that their meetings are productive in the first place, or simply not go to them. The second is that Gen Y have more desk time, are invited to fewer meetings and therefore have fewer opportunities to comment on and discuss matters of interest to them and their job.

It's not surprising that respect for the hierarchy is lower amongst this generation. It's not that they are disrespectful, just that they don't show deference for deference's sake. They talk to a "person", not a "position". As long as they are polite, there is nothing wrong with that.

Rookie Buster

Gen Y talk to a "person", not a "position". As long as they are polite, there is nothing wrong with that.

Parenting

Gen Y have experienced so-called "helicopter parenting", with parents who are very involved in all aspects of their life and decision making. They are used to being told regularly how they are doing. And they have been given the confidence to believe that they have any number of possibilities open to them.

They like to work with Gen X and Boomers, who can offer good mentoring skills, because they want to continue the attention and mentoring that they had from their parents.

Technology

Here is a generation that has grown up with the internet and technology. They are used to having access to information and people via the internet and social networking sites. The world – including the world of work – has become more democratic and transparent because of that.

They arrive at the workplace with the ability to use digital technologies, and they expect to be able to use the latest technology at work. Sometimes they find they have more advanced technologies at home than are available to them at work. And while organizations are getting hot under the collar about whether or not to ban Facebook, Gen Ys see it as a matter of trust. Their view is that working and socializing (the two are blurred in the world of Gen Y) can be done at the coffee machine, in the café and online. "So why suddenly try and restrict me online?" they think.

They are digital natives, whereas the older generations are digital immigrants. They grew up with technology; they do not have to "translate" how it applies to their "real world" as the older generation do. It *is* the real world to them. When they want to know something, they just go to Google or find someone in their online networks who is likely to know the answer. Learning facts in school seems odd to them unless they recognize the importance of doing so – why bother learning the many things you don't need to know when you can look them up on Google?

Rookie Buster

They grew up with technology; they do not have to "translate" how it applies to their "real world".

Collaboration

Gen Y have learned to collaborate on the internet. They play games with others, sometimes on the other side of the world, and they collaborate on their homework using instant messaging or social network sites.

They share knowledge, information and news using various websites set up for the purpose – Wikipedia, flickr and of course Facebook status updates.

Collaboration is the norm for them. So when Goldcorp, a gold mining company, decided to share its data, knowledge and maps with the world and offered a prize of $500,000 for the best estimates of the location of gold, many people in this hitherto very secretive industry thought the Goldcorp CEO had gone mad. But the result was amazing, as some of the best minds in the world applied themselves to the challenge. The result? The company found a lot more gold and went from a $100 million to a $9 billion company.

Open-sourcing opens problems and possibilities up to anyone,

16   anywhere in the world. Gen Y are used to that way of looking at the world – their mindset is collaborative, not competitive. And this clearly affects how they work with others and their relationships with their employers and consumers (there's more on consumers in Chapter 9).

Communication

Gen Y are used to constant communication. They like instant messaging and applications like Twitter where they can post messages about what they are doing in real-time, as well as find out what their friends are doing too. And they like to be able to find out whether any of their friends are nearby. The media they use has shaped their communication styles. Their media is instant and always "on".

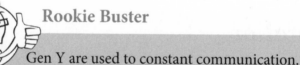

Rookie Buster

Gen Y are used to constant communication.

They get the news that they are interested in delivered to their laptops or mobile devices so that they can choose the content they want and access it when they want it. It is not that they don't use print media; they do. But their view of the world of communications is as a "stream" of information (newspapers, Google Alerts, blogs, online news, etc.). They dip into that stream when they want and need to. One of my Gen Y colleagues told me, "I skim the free paper on the bus in the morning for the headlines that interest me, I get to work and check what my favourites are Twittering about, I may check out some of those links, I have a look at my personalized news page and then go back to any of them as I need to throughout the day."

This style of using media is in contrast to Gen X and Boomers, whose approach is more like moving between pools of media instead of dipping into a stream. That is, they will sit down and do their emails for an hour, read *The Economist* on a Saturday morning, and *The Times* on the way to work. Gen X and Boomers tend to be controlled by media and when they "have" to do certain things, whereas Gen Y have control over it and when they want to use it.

Working style

Gen Y can often appear to be chaotic in their style.

They often know more than their manager about the content of their job, and there is a blurring of their work and life. Why would they want to work 9–5? Their view is that surely the most important thing is that they deliver the goods.

The world of work is more complex. One size does not fit all (actually it probably never did, but we acted as if it did because it made life easier). Boomers and Generation X put up with this standardized approach to employment and people policies. Generation Y is less willing to do so. They are not used to standardization – they can customize their mobile phones, their ethical trainers and their clothing, so why would they want to accept standardization in the workplace when individuality and expressing themselves is so important to them?

Coach's notes

Checklist: 5 steps to understanding Generation Y

1. Think about your own (conscious or unconscious) prejudices – do you see Gen Y as a problem, or are you embracing them as an opportunity?
2. Don't make assumptions about individuals – ask people from this generation what's important to them and how they like to work.
3. Don't generalize – the types of Gen Y who are attracted to your sector or organization may not be typical Gen Ys and/or may be different from those attracted to other sectors.
4. Don't judge them on their behaviour – ask them why they do things in the way they do – chances are that their intentions are good. Always ask questions to understand the behaviour you see before you judge it or jump to conclusions.
5. Show an interest in how they work – you may learn some new ways of doing things.

Go for it! The key to getting the best out of Gen Y is first to understand them. Once you understand where they are coming from and why they act the way they do you will start to see that they are not deliberately setting out to annoy the hell out of the older generation.

Having a motivated and energized workforce has great benefits. They have different perspectives on the world, and innovation only happens when different perspectives are brought to bear on an issue.

But perhaps one of the greatest benefits that Gen Y bring to organizations is that they can help you to respond to and meet the needs of Gen Y consumers.

20

Notes

Notes

The world that Gen Y has grown up in is so different in many ways to the world that the X-ers and Boomers grew up in. One of the major differences is technology and what that means for the way that young people today communicate.

Communication today is instant, person-to-person and global. As a result, Gen Y's communication behaviours can appear to be alien to the rest of us.

This chapter will explain why Gen Y communicate the way they do, and how you can communicate with them to get the results you want. It will also cover the key differences in communication styles between Gen Y and the other generations.

CHAPTER 2

Communicating with Gen Y

What shapes how Gen Y communicates?

Remember that their communication behaviours are shaped by the technology that they grew up with:

- They have never heard an engaged tone – phones go straight to voicemail, so they are not used to not being able to at least leave a message for someone.
- They can contact someone wherever they are – that can make them appear impatient.
- All of the tools they use allow and encourage instant responses. The idea that someone would communicate with them and not want a response is alien to them, whereas to Boomers and Gen X communication is not necessarily a two-way process.
- They use collaborative technologies in play and school, so find it strange when they can't do the same at work.
- Their phone or mobile device is not just a phone – it's their watch, their music player, camera and notepad.

24
- They are used to being able to access information on-demand and without moving from their desk by using Google and websites like Wikipedia. This means they may miss out on other sources of knowledge and information, such as talking to older colleagues in the workplace.
- They are used to being able to choose to receive only the information they are interested in, so are quick to hit the delete button when unwelcome communications come in. This can be very annoying to older colleagues who expect them to read whatever they are sent.
- They use different communications media for different purposes. Email tends to be for work; messaging and Facebook for their personal lives. But they do send birthday cards too! In other words, they choose the method that they judge to be appropriate to the messages and the context.
- It is sometimes assumed that their use of instant messaging technology means that they are conditioned into expecting instant responses. This is true only when the situation demands it. In fact, Boomers and Gen X are probably more likely to expect an instant response, and that can be related to power – "I am important so you must reply to me quickly."

Rookie Buster

The idea that someone would communicate with them and not want a response is alien to them.

What is important when communicating with Gen Y?

Honest communication is essential. Gen Y can see through spin a mile off. They have grown up in an age of corporate scandal and decline in the public's trust of business. They do not fall for corporate messaging and spin in the same way that Gen X and Boomers did. It's not that we were naive – it's just that we believed what we were told by company bosses. Gen Y have learned that bosses cannot always be believed.

Gen Y could have turned out to be very cynical, but they haven't. They are just savvy, and they want and demand honest communication. Authenticity, transparency and honesty are essential when communicating with Gen Y, whether you are their boss, mentor, an advertising agency or a company.

Rookie Buster

Authenticity, transparency and honesty are essential when communicating with Gen Y.

What is the best style of communicating with Gen Y?

It's no surprise that Gen Y don't respond well to formal, "corporate" speak. However, you need to guard against trying too hard to be informal, as you run the risk of sounding like a forty-year-old vicar trying to be trendy!

The key is to be honest and straightforward, and this lends itself to a natural style of writing, not a formal one. Even if your writing style is not exactly what they like, they will appreciate that you are not trying to be something you are not. Advertisers understand this, and the new

26 wave of adverts is much more direct and honest. Authenticity really is important to Gen Y. So, for example, don't try to copy how you think they write – in abbreviated text-message speak, for example. The best advice when communicating with Gen Y in writing is to write how you speak – and very few people speak in formal, corporate language.

Ideally, have someone write for you whose language is accessible and straightforward, and this will improve communications with all the generations. Use writers who can write naturally and informally – if your natural writing style is formal, trying to be informal will sound unauthentic.

Rookie Buster

Use writers who can write naturally and informally – if your natural writing style is formal, trying to be informal will sound unauthentic.

Communication has to be a two-way process

The ideal way of communicating with Gen Y is to make it a two-way process. Of course that is the best way of communicating with anyone. One-way communication is not communication at all; it is a transmission. Many organizations have developed a bad habit of believing that if they tell people something (in the CEO's quarterly message, content on the intranet or team briefings, for example) that they are communicating. It only counts as communication if it is a dialogue.

Gen X and Boomers more readily accept one-way communication because that is what they are used to. And the world of work that they have inhabited is one where you know your place in the hierarchy, and engaging in dialogue with people above you in the hierarchy is only

OK if you have a valid reason or are invited to do so. Gen Y inhabit a much more democratic world – the world of the internet. They are used to being able to communicate with all sorts of people via email, blogs and social networking sites. One-way communication or messaging is an alien and weird concept to them. Communicating with Gen Y is a two-way process. They assume that if you communicate with them you are inviting a response.

Rookie Buster

Communicating with Gen Y is a two-way process. They assume that if you communicate with them you are inviting a response.

How often should I communicate with Gen Y?

Bearing in mind that communication needs to be two-way, it seems odd to then think of frequency. The technologies that Gen Y are used to using allow them to have instant communication. Email is too slow now; they use instant messaging instead. And it doesn't matter whether they are out for lunch or sitting at their desk, they expect to be able to send and receive messages. There is no set frequency that is right. Just keep them informed and communicate as frequently as necessary.

In terms of messages that your organization might want to send out, instead of an email or passive intranet site, consider a blog – that way they can ask

28 questions and start a discussion. If you are worried about the time this might waste – well, it would be wasted anyway, but they would be just talking to one another about it instead of addressing you directly. So communicate using a blog or wiki instead of by mass emails.

Communicating via a blog can also do wonders for increasing trust and engagement – they are more likely to believe that you care about what they have to say if you open yourself up to questions, dialogue and challenge.

Rookie Buster

Communicate using a blog or wiki instead of mass emails.

What shall I communicate?

Often organizations fall into the trap of only communicating what is important to them, not what is important to their employees. The obvious thing to do is find out what people want to know about. If you use an effective two-way communications medium like a blog then you allow them to tell you.

Different things are important to different people, and it is easy to assume that what is important to one group is also important to others. HR professionals usually don't segment their audience in the same way as marketing professionals do. They treat their employees as though they are all the same. So inevitably some people will be receiving messages about subjects that they are simply not interested in. For example, Boomers may be very interested in getting regular updates on the performance of the organization's pension scheme. Your Gen Y employees are less likely to be interested in that, but perhaps more likely to want to know about what opportunities there are for training programmes or job rotation. Make sure you communicate on subjects that are important to Gen Y as well as to the other generations.

Rookie Buster

Make sure you communicate on subjects that are important to Gen Y as well as to the other generations.

Dos and don'ts

Don't invade their social spaces

Some organizations try and communicate with potential and actual employees via Facebook and other social networking sites. I would advise treading carefully with this. An organization trying to "befriend" someone on Facebook is the equivalent for Gen Y of a stranger trying to join in your conversation when you are having a drink with friends in a pub. It is their space and should be treated respectfully – and you certainly should only enter into conversation with them via these sites if you are certain that you have something of interest to say to them or there is something in it for them.

Don't blog with the intention of advertising or selling

Gen Y will see right through it and you will not be forgiven. Trying to disguise the fact that you are actually selling to them rather than genuinely communicating is dishonest, and Gen Y will not tolerate it.

Don't use spin

Gen Y's spin-detectors are pretty sophisticated. If you can't be totally open and honest in your communication then it is best not to say anything at all. Corporate brochures should have less gloss and be to the point. Many Gen Ys have told me that they don't believe what corporate brochures say. Rather they go on Facebook and find someone who works for the company in question to find out what they are really like. One company recently told me that they don't allow their graduates to use Facebook as they (the company) like to control what they discuss. I went on to Facebook and found 30 groups that their employees had set up – all had the company name in their title and some

30 had hundreds of members. They were discussing all sorts of issues including publishing the questions they had been asked in interview, asking for help to find accommodation when they were being relocated, and criticizing the company's policies.

The point is that organizations cannot control what their employees say about them on websites. Trying to stop them is pointless and can cause antagonism.

Appeal to the emotions as well as the intellect

It's important to provide more than just logic and rationale in your communications. Communication always works better if you can engage someone's emotions as well as their intellect. Gen Y are as concerned about whether something feels right and is appealing as they are about whether the logic stands up. In fact that is most probably true of all generations, but the X-ers and Boomers were conditioned that they had to have a solid, rational explanation for something and were actively encouraged to keep their feelings and intuition out of the world of work.

Be prepared to have the "risky" conversations

Gen Ys tend to bring up topics that management would really rather not discuss. Such as asking for the rationale of having to work 9–5 (when there isn't any sound rationale!). This can be uncomfortable for Boomers and Gen X, but on the positive side, it can encourage those sorts of conversations which, if handled properly, can be very healthy.

Generational differences in communication styles

Different preferences

Gen Ys spend a lot of time communicating using technology. They are always connected and communicating via their computer or mobile device. They even play with their friends remotely using web-based games. They probably spend less face-to-face time than their older colleagues do on an average day. That is not to say that they are no good at face-to-face communication, but they sometimes may miss the finer cues and subtleties. And their natural tendency is to use technology to contact colleagues rather than going to talk to them or phoning them.

Trust

Gen Ys are used to being able to communicate and connect quickly, if not instantly. They have learned to trust people online, based on whether they keep their promise as an eBay seller or write product reviews that are reliable and honest. They are therefore used to being able to make fairly quick decisions about who to trust. They may need help to understand that older colleagues take longer to trust someone and possibly are even wary of the web and worried about how "secure" it is. Building trusting relationships at work is something that most X-ers and Boomers probably take longer over than Gen Ys expect to.

Rookie Buster

Building trusting relationships at work is something that most X-ers and Boomers probably take longer over than Gen Ys expect to.

32   Each of the generations can help each other. Gen Y can teach the X-ers and Boomers about the latest technologies, and Gen Y can learn the art of face-to-face communication. Each generation has some adapting and bending to do to realize that one medium is not better than another, it's simply a question of the effectiveness of different media in different situations and for different audiences.

Power

Boomers and Gen X are used to a working world in which their employers had the power because they could control how much and what information was released to the workers. Information can no longer be restricted nor its release controlled. The internet has democratized the workplace. Gen Y cannot understand a world of work in which those at the top of the hierarchy have access to more information than anyone else. It doesn't make sense to them. If Gen Y cannot get information from their bosses, they will go to the internet or go to someone outside the organization. The internet of course makes it easy to send information outside the company walls – one press of a button and a confidential email is gone in a second. And if employees get really upset with their employers they can blog about it, write about it on Facebook or discuss it in chat rooms.

Employers still act as if they have control over their information, but of course they don't. If they ban Facebook access at work, their people can still access it via their own personal mobile devices. All the talk in 2008 about Facebook – whether it should be banned in the workplace, which companies had banned it, the effect on the employees and so on – seemed pointless. Companies were focusing on the wrong thing. The real issue was whether they trusted their people not to spend too much time on non-work activities. People can spend time socializing at work, whether it is at the coffee machine, in the outside smokers' area or on the phone. It just so happens that the use of Facebook and other websites can be monitored by company IT departments.

It is not that Gen Y want to buck the system; it is simply that they have grown up with the internet, and if you have a computer you have

as much access to information as anyone else. It does not make sense
to them that companies would want to restrict access. So if you need
to restrict access to information, explain why – and make sure it's a
good reason.

Rookie Buster

If you need to restrict access to information, explain
why – and make sure it's a good reason.

Conflict

The older generations are used to one-way communication – typically
the management sending messages via memo, the CEO's quarterly
address, and latterly email and intranet. These one-way communication methods avoid conflict, because there is no easy route through
which to challenge or question. But in the world of Web 2.0, the media
for communication are designed for discourse; the expectation is that
you can comment on whatever the other person is saying. This opens
up the possibility of conflict, because people can disagree and others
can rally round and join in the "protests". Groups of people can (and
do) effectively campaign for or against certain arguments. This can be
very uncomfortable for Gen X and Boomers, who are not used to
others being able to challenge openly in this way, and it is particularly
uncomfortable if it is senior people who are being challenged.

A natural reaction from the older generations is to try and control
the argument, to stick to the company line whether or not they believe
in it, and to try and avoid getting into dialogue about tricky issues. This
makes things worse. The best way to handle such discussions when
they arise is to engage with people as openly and honestly as possible.
And remember that just because the one-way media limited the possibility of dialogue and disagreement, it didn't mean that all your
employees agreed with you. They were probably chattering at the water

34 cooler instead. Uncomfortable as it is, at least with Web 2.0 technologies you know what people are saying and have the chance to have a discussion with them. That has to be better than having a festering mass of unexpressed opinion with all the damage that can give rise to.

Rookie Buster

Remember that just because the one-way media limited the possibility of dialogue and disagreement, it didn't mean that all your employees agreed with you.

Coach's notes

1. Understand your audience and what's important to them.
2. Be honest – they see through corporate spin.
3. Communicate informally and regularly.
4. Make communication a two-way process.
5. Don't try and write in a Gen Y way – you may end up sounding like a forty-year-old vicar trying to be trendy.
6. Think about what they want to know, not just what you want to tell them.
7. Don't tell, involve.
8. Don't dictate, explain.
9. Communicate values as well as facts.
10. Consider using a blog rather than email to communicate important messages.

Go for it! Hopefully this chapter has given you insight into why Gen Y is sometimes hard to understand in terms of the ways that they communicate. You now understand why they communicate as they do and the profound effect that technology has had on their communications behaviour. This means that you can discuss with them your different styles, and you can explain why those differences exist. This in itself will help to create positive communications between you and them. And it also opens up the door for you to learn from each other – they can teach you the new technologies so that you get ahead of the game, while you can teach them about how communication works in the organizational setting and help them communicate easily with all generations.

Time and time again Gen Y colleagues, friends and clients have told me that what they want most from their older co-workers is to learn. This is a golden opportunity for you to mentor them – they will love it!

Notes

Demographic changes mean that competition for good people is going to increase. Finding and keeping the right people has never been more important. Generation Y are a talented group of people who are going to become more and more in demand as the war for talent gets tougher around the world. The companies who know how to attract and select the best Gen Ys will certainly have a competitive advantage.

In this chapter you will learn about why attracting and recruiting Gen Y is different from attracting and recruiting Gen X and Boomers. And you will find out the best ways of getting the Gen Y employees you need.

CHAPTER 3

How to attract and recruit the right Gen Ys for you

What attracts Gen Y is different from what attracted X-ers and Boomers

Gen X were lured into a job by the prospect of being able to get on, by the pay and benefits and security. They are loyal to themselves and their career and wanted to see what their career ladder would look like before they joined a company.

Boomers looked for fulfilment and status, and they wanted to work for a company they could feel loyal to. They were building their careers in the days when working for one organization for life was the norm, when changing jobs every few years looked flighty, and when most organizations had long service awards – the assumption being that the longer you stayed with a company, the better it was.

Gen Y is looking for work that they will learn from, that will help them to grow and build their portfolio of knowledge. They want to do work that is meaningful to them, and they want to learn from their older colleagues.

40 It is important to remember these differences in values and attitudes if you are going to be able to attract Gen Y. They will not respond to the sorts of "lures" that X-ers and Boomers respond to.

Rookie Buster

Gen Y is looking for work that they will learn from, that will help them to grow and build their portfolio of knowledge.

What doesn't attract Gen Ys at all (but companies still put on their "benefits" list)

Many companies carry on acting as though what attracted people twenty years ago will attract them today. Either it doesn't occur to them that the different generations want different things, or they are hoping against hope that by telling people that what they have to offer really are benefits, their potential hires will be convinced.

Here are the most common benefits I see in job advertisements that really *don't* attract Gen Ys (apart from those who are more like Gen Xs and so go for the more traditionally run sectors):

- Pension schemes.
- Company cars (especially uninteresting to Gen Ys working in cities).
- Childcare/childcare vouchers.
- Eye test vouchers (scraping the bottom of the barrel, this one – even if they wear glasses, will they really see this as a benefit?).
- Share schemes (may be interesting to the few twenty-somethings who will trade cash for savings).

What does attract Gen Y

Some of the benefits that Gen Y really do see as benefits are not as costly as some of the items listed above. Perhaps senior managers assume for that reason that they are not valued benefits. They include:

- Interest-free travel loans (especially valued in big cities).
- Interest-free loans for bicycle purchase (great for cities and for those who care about the environment).
- Gym, or gym membership paid.
- Personal development and training.
- A good manager or mentor (this is extremely high on the list for many Gen Ys – they really want to learn from their older colleagues).
- A chance to try other jobs or learn new things via a job-rotation scheme.
- Flexible working hours so that they can keep up their other hobbies and interests.

It would be a good idea to put benefits on your website – but put them all, not just the ones that the senior managers consider to be a valuable benefit. The younger generation may value a lot of what you can offer, but they need to know about it.

Some companies hardly mention the benefits of working with them at all, and merely say something like "You will receive the benefits that you would normally expect from a leading organization." Apart from being plain lazy, that is such a missed opportunity to sell the company – after all, how are graduates supposed to know what benefits they can expect from a leading organization? Find out what your Gen Ys consider to be benefits – you may already be offering them, but just failing to tell people when you are trying to attract them. According to the talentsmoothie research, company websites are the most important source of information for graduates when they are looking for a job. So you need to make sure yours works hard for you. Think of the vacancies section of your website as an excellent marketing opportunity, and make it work for you.

Rookie Buster

Find out what your Gen Ys consider to be benefits –
you may already be offering them, but just failing to tell
people when you are trying to attract them.

Recruiters' biggest mistake

All the mistakes I mention in this chapter are of course a problem, but
one of the biggest mistakes I see recruiters of Gen Y make is *making
promises they cannot deliver.*

Some of them *know* that the promises made in the glossy brochures
they give to candidates cannot be fulfilled. One of the most cited
reasons for leaving a company within the first couple of years is that it
wasn't delivering on its promise and/or it wasn't as good as it was made
out to be during the recruitment process.

It is tempting to over-sell to get the right people in, but it is a short-
term fix to a problem and will create other problems later. Sure, it is
difficult if you know that the company culture will pose a problem to
Gen Ys, and that they will find it stifling and old fashioned, as others
have before them – but to pretend the company culture is different
from what it is will not only lead to people leaving but could also
damage your employer brand.

Rookie Buster

To pretend the company culture is different from what
it is will not only lead to people leaving but could also
damage your employer brand.

So what can you do when you know that there are flaws in the company that might put off potentially good candidates? The most important thing is to be honest. That is not to say you have to criticize the company. Nor does it mean you have to regale candidates with what you believe to be problems about the company and its culture (for one thing, what you perceive as a problem may not be a problem to others). But you can answer questions honestly. For example, if a candidate asks you what the management style is like in the department you are recruiting for, you can answer that some people find it OK and others don't. And you can genuinely add that to experience and learn to handle a range of different styles is a good learning opportunity. People can learn from having inadequate managers, if only to learn what not to do themselves.

You can also tell your candidate that one of the things you look for in new young recruits is the chance to change some of the more unhelpful parts of the current organizational culture.

As long as you honestly believe what you are telling them, you can turn a potential reason for them to turn down the job into a reason why they might take it. A 26-year-old who I mentor has recently taken a job in an organization with a very old-fashioned culture because he wants to build up his experience of implementing change in a tougher environment than the ones he has worked in before. When they hired him they were honest about the challenges and he consciously decided to go there because of these challenges. So be honest about the upsides and downsides (as you see them) of coming to work for your company. And remember that what you may regard to be a downside, others may not.

Rookie Buster

Be honest about the upsides and downsides (as you see them) of coming to work for your company. And remember that what you may regard to be a downside, others may not.

44 *The best selection methods for Gen Y*

Current methods are biased

Current methods of attraction and recruitment can be inadvertently biased towards the older generations. That's not surprising, because they were devised with those people in mind. The values, attitudes, approaches and skills-sets of the younger generation differ markedly from those of Boomers and Gen X. One of the ways that Gen Y differ from other generations is their tendency towards, and preference for, collaborative working. This is in large part due to their use of technology. The implications of this are changes in the way they work, communicate and learn.

Many organizations use competency frameworks to assess potential new recruits, but these changes in preferred ways of working may not be reflected in current competency frameworks and other assessment criteria. The majority of competency frameworks were devised by Boomers and X-ers, as were psychometric and other tests. Existing norm groups are of course made up of Boomers and X-ers. For many companies, competency frameworks and psychological tests play a crucial part in a number of HR processes, including selection and recruitment. However, the competency benchmarks that companies are judging their people against could be out of date or at least in need of examination in today's context and in relation to the contemporary workforce. For example, norm groups of senior managers in large corporations are commonly used. The assumption is that these are good, or at least useful, comparators, and that the up-and-coming talent inside a company should aspire to be like those who are running companies today. Gen Y or no Gen Y, we need to re-evaluate what we want from our future leaders and whether what we want is the same as what we have now. That aside, current leadership styles are

arguably still predominantly based on command and control. That is   45
not to say that these styles are ineffective in some contexts. However,
Gen Y are inherently more collaborative in their working style.

Selecting for out-of-date skills?

It's a fair bet that when Gen Y are in charge of companies (and they are
of the age where they are getting into junior and middle management
positions already), the prevailing leadership style will be collaborative
and enabling, not controlling and commanding. But many organizations are, perhaps unintentionally, judging a future generation of
leaders against an outdated model, and thus perhaps mistakenly
excluding good future leaders from their talent pool or high-flier
development programmes.

Inevitably we look at the world through our own filters and from a
standpoint of the prevailing paradigm. The dominant organizational/
leadership paradigm for many years has been a hierarchical one that is
based on the assumption that people need to be controlled and monitored. Evidence of this is the 9–5 working hours culture (flexible working
is still not the norm – many companies struggle to trust their employees
enough to manage outcomes rather than the process) and power-based
organizational cultures. Gen Y want something different. They are a
generation that has grown up with the internet and technology. They
are used to having access to information and people via the
internet and social networking sites. The world has
become more democratic and transparent because
of that, and this includes the world of work. They
are less concerned about the hierarchy, and more
concerned about getting to the right person,
whoever that person may be. All this means that it is
time to review the very assumptions and founda-
tions upon which some existing attraction and
recruitment approaches are based. If you are recruiting, you need to make sure that you are totally clear about
what you are looking for – and that you are not just looking

46 for the same as you have always looked for before out of habit.

Rookie Buster

If you are recruiting, you need to make sure that you are totally clear about what you are looking for – and that you are not just looking for the same as you have always looked for before out of habit.

What should you be judging people on?

Companies typically judge potential hires solely on their ability to do the job. They may or not find out whether people actually *want* to do the job. They take this as a given. Ideally of course, those we hire really do want to do the job. But what we should in fact be finding out is whether they would *love* to do it. You need to select people who love to do the job, not those who are merely able to do it.

Rookie Buster

You need to select people who love to do the job, not those who are merely able to do it.

Doing a job that you love to do plays to your strengths and leads to better performance as well as more satisfaction. Generation Y are much more attuned to this. They have typically been brought up to expect that they can aspire to doing a job that they love. HR people and managers have been well trained to focus lots of time and effort on figuring out people's "gaps" and looking for their "development needs". However, fantastic performers play to their strengths. Research shows that doing work that they love and playing to their strengths were the No. 1 factors in why graduates chose the employers they do, and in their motivation when they started work. Whilst Gen X might accept a job that they are 50 per cent happy with, Gen Y probably expect more than 80 per cent satisfaction from theirs.

It is nothing new that the best performers are those who have the capability to do the job as well as *loving* to do the job. All of us would prefer to have a job that we love to do, but Boomers and Gen X probably don't expect that always to be possible.

Why do they need a degree?

I have had many conversations with graduate recruiters in which I have asked why they are restricting themselves to hiring people with 2:1s and above, and, in some cases, why the people they are hiring need a degree at all. I work with some super-bright non-graduates who are doing graduate level jobs or running their own enterprises.

Apart from some professions where the skills they learn in a degree are essential (medicine or architecture, for example), there is no good answer to that question. For most jobs, the degree the person has studied is probably unrelated to the job, and a degree is not an indicator of intelligence, nor is it an indicator of someone's ability to do the job. So why do organizations insist on degrees? The real answer is that it makes their life easier. Asking for a degree is a bulk sifting mechanism: it screens out hundreds of other people (some of whom might be superb hires) and so cuts down the number of applications someone has to read. It's as simple as that.

I work with some super-bright, committed non-graduates. One of them, Lamorna, you can read about below. Another passed the aptitude tests to get into a software development company that almost exclusively employs graduates from Oxford and Cambridge universities, and another is 23 and has worked his way up from a call centre job to UK sales manager since he started work. There are many talented young people out there, but companies miss out on them because of their fixation with degrees.

Rookie Buster

There are many talented young people out there, but companies miss out on them because of their fixation with degrees.

Of course some sort of bulk sifting mechanism is needed. The first step is to be clear about the sort of person that you want to hire. Then you can devise a bulk, online set of questionnaires testing for the characteristics you want – you may want an intelligence test, an emotional intelligence assessment and a strengths assessment. The sifting can be automated according to your needs. Rather than restricting your recruitment to the country you are in, this means you can go global in your recruitment and therefore massively extend your potential pool of candidates. In the future, when talent shortages really start to bite, this will be the only way to ensure that you get the up-and-coming workforce you need.

Lamorna is an example of someone very bright who did not get into university and could not get a graduate level job as a result. She eventually landed a job for a big, high-profile sports sponsorship organization: only later did she find out that the boss of this organization had not wanted to hire her as he thought she was too young to be able to handle the responsibility of coordinating high-risk sporting events and handling the not uncommon crises that occurred. At last she had an opportunity to prove herself. She quickly found her feet, did an excellent job and after a couple of years was poached by the competition. Incidentally, the boss who had been so against her appointment became her biggest fan and remains so.

At this stage she was still only 21, and by now had a lot of experience under her belt, a good network of contacts and ever-increasing confidence. She started applying for graduate level jobs again, but found that she could not even get through the online process, because if you don't complete certain sections of the form you cannot move into the following sections.

By this time she had acquired many skills and lots of experience, and she had a clear idea of where her strengths lay. And she was ready for her next big work challenge. She is a determined person and she pointed out to some of the companies that she was probably a better prospect than some graduates, as she had a number of years' experience in demanding jobs, had acquired a whole load of useful expertise "and could provide stellar references". However, she still could not get through their process, and even when she determinedly badgered prospective employers with phone calls, no one would even give her a chance. So she decided to set up a social enterprise organization with a friend. At the time of writing, the enterprise is two years old and this year they are on target to raise £1.2 million for charity. Both the organization and the young women have won a number of awards, and she is now on demand on the speaker circuit.

Clearly the organizations she approached missed out on a very talented individual because of their screening process. Think about what is really important for the job you are offering: is a degree really necessary? By being really clear about what you need, you can target excellent hires much more precisely. Excuse the analogy, but why use a blunderbuss to hit a moving target if you can use a high-powered sniper rifle instead?

Interviewing Gen Ys

Until fairly recently, recruiters mainly focused on finding out why they should be employing the person sitting in front of them for the job. These days it's much more of a two-way process. The balance of power has shifted. Good candidates are keen on checking out not just what they can do for a company, but what a company can do for them. And that's fair enough. Really good employees deserve a fair exchange for their time, labour, knowledge and skill.

Gen Y ask all sorts of questions at interview that their older co-workers might want to ask but would never dream of actually saying. Questions like:

- What development will you give me?

50
- Which latest technologies will I have access to at work?
- What support will my manager give me in my job?
- Why do I have to work from 9 to 5.30? I like to work from home sometimes and the technology allows it.
- I have a hobby that's important to me, and I will need to take some afternoons off to travel, but will make up the work at the weekends. Is that OK?

Rookie Buster

Gen Y ask all sorts of questions at interview that their older co-workers might want to ask but would never dream of actually saying.

I recently spoke to a recruiter from a company in an industry that is not perceived to be particularly appealing to graduates. She was telling me what trouble they were having hiring good engineering graduates. That week, however, one of their preferred candidates had accepted a job with them. They were delighted, but then the candidate rang to say he was a musician as well as an engineer and he needed time to rehearse, so could he renegotiate his contract to a four-day instead of a five-day week. The company in question were appalled that he should ask such a thing and said no. So basically they could have had a good person for four days a week, but ended up not having him at all. Companies are going to have to start being more flexible and imaginative in their approach to hiring, because it is becoming more and more likely that the good people will start to make such requests!

Coach's notes

- Find out what your target recruits value as benefits, and put them on your website.
- Use technologies such as chatrooms and blogs that allow candidates to have a dialogue with you about the opportunities, what your organization is like, etc.
- Make sure you are hiring what you really need for today's world and tomorrow's world too – don't keep unquestioningly hiring the same types of people.
- Don't assume that all generations want the same benefits – different benefits appeal to different generations (and of course there is variation within the generations too).
- Move on from asking "Can they do the job?" and ask "Can they do the job and will they *love* to do it?" Ask them what they love doing and what they are passionate about. Observe their body language when they are talking to you – passion shows. Hiring for passion as well as competence will bring you the strongest candidates.
- Think about any "restrictive" working practices you have that may put Gen Y off – for example, why do they have to work 9 to 5? Employers who can be more flexible will have their choice of more candidates.
- Really listen to the questions the candidates are asking at interview. They are clues to the sorts of things you can do to make your organization more attractive to good people.
- Think about what skills are needed to take your organization forward – skills like collaborative working, listening well and building trusting relationships and the ability to network well.

Go for it! There are many great Gen Y candidates out there, but because of the ageing global population, they will be in greater and greater demand (even taking account of graduates from India and China). You will be able to compete well for the best talent if you simply take a look at some of your hiring practices and make the simple changes suggested in this chapter.

It doesn't actually take much to get a reputation as a forward-thinking organization. It's amazing how a few small steps can take you to a position of being "best in class".

Notes

Keeping people motivated and engaged in their work has been an age-old challenge for organizations and managers. Just when some of them are starting to get to grips with how to do this, along comes Gen Y. And many of the rules we have learned go out of the window.

Gen Y are motivated by different things than their colleagues from the other generations, and engaging them means really understanding that they are different from Gen X and the Boomers. Any manager these days needs to understand this if they are to hire the best, encourage them to work productively, keep hold of them and get a reputation as a place where Gen Y really do want to work.

Read this chapter and take a look inside the mind of Gen Y. It could be the key to your competitive advantage.

CHAPTER 4

Motivating and engaging Gen Y

Golden Rule No. 1 – don't assume

The most important piece of advice about Gen Y is not to assume that they are like the other generations. Don't even assume that they are like one another – there are variations within Gen Y too. It is crucial to find out what engages them. And don't assume you know what keeps your Gen Y employees motivated – ask them! It's as simple as that. When you start asking you will definitely be surprised by the answers (often pleasantly so, as they are motivated by some things that are far easier to give than you might imagine).

Rookie Buster

Don't assume you know what keeps your Gen Y employees motivated – ask them! It's as simple as that.

56   *What keeps Gen Y engaged at work?*

Doing work that they love

In no small part because of the messages they have received from their Boomer parents, Gen Y are conditioned into believing that they should go after work that they really love. In recent years popular psychology has become much more mainstream, and there are hundreds of books encouraging people to "do the work they were born to do" and such-like. Gen X and Boomers did not grow up in that context. Gen Y did, and good for them that they believe that it is important to do work that you really love. So many older people don't. (Some of the Boomer mentors I speak to who mentor Gen Y have told me that they find it unbelievable – and unrealistic sometimes – that young people today expect to be able to do work that they love. The Boomers see it as a luxury you achieve if you are lucky.)

The good news is that Gen Y don't expect employers to somehow miraculously come up with a job for them that they love. They take responsibility for finding the job themselves. But what they do want and expect is help from the older generations to find out what kind of work is right for them and how to make sure that they can mould their job so that they love it. For example, a Gen Y who I was mentoring through his job search found a company that really inspired him. He knew that he would only be able to get an entry level job there on the IT helpdesk, but he also believed that he would make it into something he loved. Indeed he did – his love was solving problems and sharing what he learned with others. All of the jobs that he has had since have fulfilled his needs, because he is clear about what those needs are and he figures out ways of meeting those needs in the roles he takes on. Talk to your Gen Ys about what they love doing and help them to think through how they might use what they love in order to make their job fulfilling.

Rookie Buster

Talk to your Gen Ys about what they love doing and help them to think through how they might use what they love in order to make their job fulfilling.

Working with highly engaged people

This one can be trickier. Imagine a scenario in which the Gen Y is working in a team of disillusioned colleagues. Disaster. We all enjoy working with engaged, enthusiastic people, and it can bring us down if we don't. Paying attention to this is important, and can mean the difference between a Gen Y staying or leaving. If they are assigned to a team that is not particularly engaged, try sitting them next to a team that is, so at least that rubs off on them.

Making sure they have a good mentor is another way of mitigating the effects of "toxic" co-workers. The mentor can help to keep them boosted and on-track. Similarly, giving them opportunities to stay connected with the other Gen Ys in the organization through social events is important.

Good induction

Good induction starts long before the person's first day in their job. It starts with your first communication with them. That is when they start to learn about and get a feel for the organization.

So often, organizations miss this opportunity to really engage Gen Ys from the off. Induction programmes are typically one-hit days on which lots of information is downloaded to them, senior managers are paraded in front of them and they are told

58 what they can and cannot do. We would do well to learn from the marketing world when it comes to induction. Sure, it is a chance to impart important information – but it can be done in an engaging and fun way. Gen Ys don't like to sit in a room for hours being talked at and suffering death by PowerPoint (let's face it, who does?). They want and expect a two-way interaction. They want to be entertained as well as educated. And they are interested in talking to other people, not just the senior ones – and preferably interesting ones!

Rookie Buster

Gen Ys don't like to sit in a room for hours being talked at and suffering death by PowerPoint (let's face it, who does?).

Flexibility and understanding

The rules surrounding working hours, work location and flexible working are being challenged by Gen Y, some of them rightly so. When you think about it, the 9–5 working hours norm was appropriate and fitting for factory workers and other organizations where there was good reason for people to be at their workplace between certain times – for instance, to make efficient use of machinery. Similarly, there were days when people needed to be in the office in order to be able to discuss issues with colleagues, get guidance from their boss and have meetings. Nowadays there are many jobs that can be done from any location as long as there is an internet connection and the right technology available. Of course, no technology can completely replace face-to-face interaction, but providing managers trust their people, there are probably many of them who can work from locations other than their office. If the manager doesn't trust them, then it raises the question as to whether the company is employing the right people.

Gen Y want to know the rationale if they are told they can't do something. They won't obediently say "Oh, OK." Managing their work outputs rather than how long they are in the office means you can be much more flexible, and you will have a much more motivated workforce. If you think about it, this applies to all generations.

Rookie Buster

Gen Ys want to know the rationale if they are told they can't do something. They won't obediently say "Oh, OK."

Good management/mentoring

Gen Y are used to parents who give them a lot of attention, encouragement and feedback as to how well they are doing. Their parents tend to be very closely involved with their children (hence the term "helicopter parenting"), and certainly much more closely than the X-ers' and Boomers' parents were. So when Gen Y arrive in the workplace it's a shock to them if they get a manager who doesn't give them much attention, or gives them the wrong kind of attention (such as checking up and criticizing).

Rookie Buster

Invest in a mentoring scheme – it is a great way of making sure you hang on to and make the best of your top talent.

Not many managers like managing or are good at it. That's just the reality of organizational life. But the effects of an indifferent manager

60   on Gen Y can be mitigated if at least they have an excellent mentor who is interested in them and their progress. Invest in a mentoring scheme – it is a great way of making sure you hang on to and make the best of your top talent. Having a good manager and/or mentor can make up for so many other things that are not right. The old adage is still true – people leave managers, not organizations.

Learning and development

This is hugely important to Gen Y. They want to feel they are constantly learning new things and learning from the other generations. Career succession is for Gen Y less about a "ladder" and more about a journey of discovery and learning. The ladder is linked to promotion and status – Gen Y care less about those things and more about an inner sense of progression. And learning has to be a constant activity. The occasional training course might be important to them, but they want to learn every day. They want feedback, guidance, mentoring and coaching to help them learn. And any formal learning events that they do attend have to be fun, engaging and worthwhile.

Doing meaningful work

Gen Y want to do work that is meaningful to them. The definition of meaningful obviously varies from person to person. When someone says at an interview, "I want to do meaningful work," interviewers often fall into the trap of not checking out what the person really means by that and simply assume they want to do work that is useful to society in some way. I spoke to a graduate who was working in a bank, and his work was meaningful to him because financial institutions had such a powerful impact on the world. Another Gen Y told me that his work was meaningful to him because he took it upon himself to help new people who joined his team.

A client in a financial services company told me about a costly mistake they had made because of their assumptions about what was important to their graduates. They set up a series of days for the graduates to work in the local community. The scheme completely flopped. When they asked the graduates why, the response they got was that they wanted to do something meaningful, but would prefer to write a cheque rather than do volunteering! Don't assume that you know what someone means when they say they want to do meaningful work. Ask them the question, "What do you mean by 'meaningful'?"

Rookie Buster

Don't assume that you know what someone means when they say they want to do meaningful work.

Playing to their strengths

The best performers are those people who play to their strengths. They are also happier and more energized than they would be if they were not playing to their strengths. Gen Y are probably more aware than the older generations of what their strengths are, because they are likely to have had more feedback. Selecting people for jobs based on their strengths is obviously a good idea – they are more likely to do a good job and less likely to leave, because they will be happy in their work.

Ask people about their strengths when you are hiring them, and also when you are talking to them about their performance. That doesn't mean ignoring their weaknesses, but leveraging strengths can create exceptional performance, whereas improving weaknesses can only create acceptable performance.

62 Looking after people once the Graduate Programme ends

A common complaint from graduates is that they are effectively "dumped" and left to their own devices at the end of their (typically two-year) graduate programme. The end of the programme is one of the most vulnerable times for graduates and their companies, as this is when they leave if they do not feel taken care of. It's not about pampering or pandering. It's about providing them with some sense that they are still important to the organization, and that support is available to them. Unless they have a very good manager, an excellent way of providing them with continuity and support is to assign them a mentor. It has to be someone who really wants to do mentoring, is skilled at having top-notch conversations, and has a passion for developing people. Most mentoring programmes are totally ineffective because people have no idea how to be a mentor: they see it as a chore, neither party gets much out of it, and there is no energy or momentum. From what I hear, many mentoring schemes end up that way.

It is not difficult to set up a scheme that works. And the dividends are enormous: managers get to know their top talent really well, it is developmental for both sides, any potential problems that the young person has can be picked up and resolved before they get out of hand, and it can prevent someone from possibly leaving the organization due to lack of support. Good mentoring is an under-used and under-estimated technique for developing and engaging people. And it is a superb way of gaining a deep understanding of the talent in your organization. Top tips for setting up a mentoring scheme that works are:

- Choose mentors who really want to do the job and have a natural aptitude for it.
- Train the mentors well – and that means brilliantly well. They need to be able to have high-challenge/high-support conversations. And they need to inspire their mentee.
- Train the mentees too – they need to know how to choose a mentor who is right for them, and how to make the most of the mentoring relationship.
- Let people match themselves with people they want to work with

– good mentoring conversations can be challenging for both parties, so they have to like working together.

- Involve the participants in the design of the programme so that they own it.
- Consider a reciprocal mentoring scheme, in which the two people mentor one another. For example, a senior manager may want some help with understanding and using new technologies. The younger person may want help in understanding organizational politics and how to network. They can help each other, and it's a great way of promoting cross-generational understanding and appreciation in the workplace.

Rookie Buster

Good mentoring is an under-used and underestimated technique for developing and engaging people.

Money

Money is lower down on Gen Y's list of wants from a job than it typically is for X-ers and Boomers. It is certainly less of a statement of status. They seem prepared to take less money in order to do a job that they really want to do. For example, I have heard of Gen Ys in law firms deciding that they would rather leave and do work they wanted to do, because even the lure of very large salaries further down the line did not make up for the fact they didn't particularly enjoy the work and really didn't like the long hours they had to put in. A partner of a law firm in his forties told me he didn't like the work, the culture or the hours either, but because he earned a lot of money he found it very hard to leave. Gen Ys see their parents and colleagues in this situation and are determined not to get into it themselves.

Having said that, they will not be exploited, and even when they are doing work that they love they expect fair pay for it.

64   Networking and a chance to work collaboratively

Working collaboratively is Gen Y's natural way of working. At school, they work in teams and collaborate on projects and with homework. They like to be able to talk to others – either face-to-face or using technology. They like to be in constant communication. They are used to being able to reach out and ask for help as well as to offer help.

Rookie Buster

Gen Y like to be in constant communication. They are used to being able to reach out and ask for help as well as to offer help.

If you belong to an older generation, you are probably thinking rather enviously, "I would have liked all those things in my job too." I have found that much of what Gen Y demand, older generations would have quite liked too, but they were conditioned not to expect it. That is the difference. So addressing these issues will result not just in more engaged Gen Y workers, but also in more engaged workers of all generations.

However, there is one clear difference between what Gen X and Boomers want from work and what their Gen Y colleagues want. The older generations are still more focused on the "hygiene" factor elements of work, whereas Gen Y have come straight into the workplace expecting the hygiene factors as a given, and wanting fulfilment and self-actualization too. For example, wanting personal meaning from work is something that typically the older generations haven't started thinking about until they reach their forties. Again, they were conditioned to want and expect money, status (eventually – and if they were lucky) and security from their work. It was only as the years progressed that they might have started to think about what mattered most to them about the work they did and whether they found it fulfilling enough.

Coach's notes

Top tips for engaging your Gen Y

- Don't assume that you know what is important to them – ask them.
- Gen Y expect different things than their older co-workers do from their company and their managers – don't assume that what works for one group will work for everyone.
- Gen Y engagement is emotional, not intellectual – you need to engage them personally and individually.
- During recruitment interviews and performance conversations, talk to them about their strengths and what they love to do – having those conversations will in itself be engaging.
- If you do nothing else, set up a strong mentoring scheme – it is one of the most powerful ways of creating high engagement.
- Train managers and mentors to help Gen Ys learn – it is a skill that can be learned and honed. Managers and mentors need to be constantly helping Gen Ys to learn and to realize that they are constantly learning.

66

Go for it! So much talent is wasted in organizations because people are not fully engaged and not firing on all cylinders. Knowing how to engage Gen Y is knowing how to make the most of this valuable asset.

As you will have learned from this chapter, much of what it takes to motivate and engage Gen Y is very simple, not expensive and very powerful. Imagine if you achieved no more than a 10 per cent increase in motivation from just 10 per cent of your people – what could even that modest achievement do for customer relationships, innovation and productivity? Apply some of the ideas in this chapter and you will get way more than just a 10 per cent increase – now that's worth having!

Notes

Managing Gen Y is different from managing the other generations. Managers all over the world are struggling with managing and leading Gen Y because their attitudes and behaviours are so different from the X-ers and Boomers they have been used to managing. For many X-er and Boomer managers, Gen Y have proved to be a challenge – they struggle to understand Gen Y and to come to terms with their some-times demanding ways. This challenge is being felt by managers the world over, even in more deferential cultures such as in Asia. Gone are the days when seniority equalled unquestioned authority. In this chap-ter you will discover why Gen Y is proving so demanding, and why a different style of management is needed for them. You will learn the best ways of managing them and some simple techniques that you can apply right away.

CHAPTER 5

Managing Gen Y

Managing Gen Y – why are they so "difficult"?

I hear so many stories from organizations I work with about what a challenge Gen Y are proving to be for managers. There are far fewer stories about what a joy they are to manage! Understandably, there is a fair amount of frustration and conflict brought about by the different, styles, expectations and attitudes of the different generations in the workplace right now.

Different world/different expectations

The context in which Boomers and Gen X grew up was one where senior managers or anyone above you in the managerial hierarchy had more status, power and therefore "voice" than anyone below them. This is a largely unspoken (and often extremely unhelpful) characteristic of organizational life. Many Boomers came into the workplace at

70   a time when managers were always addressed as "Mister" (there were few female managers in senior positions), the only contact you had with management was with your own direct boss, and if other managers wanted to approach you for something they would do so via your boss. Things had not changed substantially when Gen X entered the workplace. The external symbols had changed – there was less formality and more focus on "empowerment" – but actually the unspoken, very strong power-based framework prevailed, as it still does today in many organizations.

Gen Ys usually start to realize this only when they come up against a problem. An example of this was a young woman working in a bank. Her alarm failed to go off one morning, so she arrived at work late. Instead of slipping in quietly and apologizing to the manager, she strode into the floor manager's corner office and said "Damned alarm clock didn't go off, could you just give me a quick run-down on the markets?" The manager was furious and shouted at the young woman. She couldn't understand why he was so angry, as she was being totally honest about being late, and she had asked him about the markets as she thought he would be the most knowledgeable person there and so it would be the quickest way of catching up. The young woman clearly didn't understand the rules of the game. And as we discussed in Chapter 1, neither of them understood where the other was coming from or their intentions.

You could ask why no one would think to tell graduates or warn them, so that they didn't inadvertently cause problems for themselves and others. The reason is that people are so used to the organizational systems being the way they are that they don't even think about them, let alone question them.

Rookie Buster

People are so used to the organizational systems being the way they are that they don't even think about them, let alone question them.

Gen Y grew up in a very different context to that in which their older co-workers grew up. To understand where they are coming from you need to understand that context. Here are the underlying assumptions that the Boomers/Gen X-ers and the Gen Ys have about the world of work. They are often unconscious and therefore often don't get discussed.

Boomers'/Gen X's assumptions	Gen Y's assumptions
Challenging senior managers is a career-limiting thing to do.	Challenging anyone who seems to be wrong is a natural and important thing to do.
If I want to communicate with someone higher than your boss, I discuss it with him/her first.	I should be able to communicate with whoever I need to communicate with in the organization.
If I disagree with a manager's view or decision, I only voice that disagreement if I am sure I am "safe" to do so.	If I disagree with someone, I say so.
Even if the CEO says he has an "open door" policy, it's not a good idea to say exactly what you think (unless it's positive).	The fact that the CEO has to say he has an "open door" policy is odd. I should be able to talk to whoever I like, and to email the CEO any time.
It's sensible to make sure I look good in the eyes of senior managers and "manage my reputation" with them.	Surely my results speak for themselves and that should be all that counts.
My experience of feedback is that it is usually a criticism, so I dread it. I would hesitate to give feedback to my boss even if asked.	I welcome feedback from my boss and peers so that I can keep learning.

Boomers'/Gen X's assumptions	Gen Y's assumptions
When I was younger I expected to get the boring jobs and do my time before being able to move on to more interesting work.	I have a lot to contribute and want to do so straight away.

So when the generations clash it is usually because one generation does not know that the other is playing by very different rules. If a Gen Y does something that you find unacceptable, pause and ask them what led them to do it. Invariably they will not have realized that their behaviour could be seen as unacceptable, and you will also uncover a good reason behind it.

The behaviour we see Gen Ys display – as shown above – may seem inappropriate, but the intentions behind the behaviour are good. Gen Y aren't as bolshy, disrespectful and out of order as some people say. On the contrary, some of the organizational cultures and practices that they are inadvertently challenging probably *need* challenging. Perhaps some organizations could actually benefit from updating their old-fashioned management styles.

Rookie Buster

The behaviour we see Gen Ys display may seem inappropriate, but the intentions behind the behaviour are good.

What do Gen Y want from a manager?

Here are the qualities Gen Y look for in their managers and mentors:
- Integrity.
- Honesty.

- Openness.
- Supportive style.
- Mentoring style.

The personal characteristics of their manager are important to them, as well as how they actually manage.

Integrity, openness and honesty may be high on Gen Y's agenda because they are aware of the corporate and political scandals of the last few years. They realize that not all leaders have these qualities, but don't want to be led by those who don't. They will not give their respect to a boss just because of his or her position in the company.

The four secrets to successfully managing Gen Y

1. Mentor, not manage

Really excellent mentors are worth their weight in gold. They provide guidance and support, they fill the knowledge gaps and they help their mentee to learn. This is what a good manager should do too.

The most effective way of managing Gen Y is to stop thinking of yourself as a manager and start thinking that you are a mentor. Mentoring comes up time and time again as one of Gen Y's greatest desires. They are hungry to learn and do well, and a mentor can help them learn.

Rookie Buster

The most effective way of managing Gen Y is to stop thinking of yourself as a manager and start thinking that you are a mentor.

Here's why mentoring is so important to Gen Y:

- They are used to having a much more hands-on relationship with their parents than previous generations had. Gen Y's parents are much more inclined to be closely involved with all aspects of their children's lives and decisions, and their parents give them regular feedback. This creates a need for on-tap mentoring-style relationships with important older people.
- The huge amount of information available to them at any one time via the internet means that having significant relationships with people who can guide them becomes much more important than it otherwise would. A good mentor can help his or her mentee figure out what is important and what to focus on.

To be a good mentor you need to:

- First of all ask yourself whether you *really want to be a mentor*. The best mentors really want to be mentors and have a passion for developing others. If you don't, that's OK, and you should play to your own strengths, but make sure that others are available to mentor your team. Not wanting to be a mentor is not a problem: it's pretending you do that leads to problems.
- Make sure that you and your mentee are a good match – do you like each other, do you share some of the same values? Is this person someone you would quite like to spend time with anyway?
- Build trust – this means demonstrating that the relationship is important to you by committing to it, not changing appointments, and showing an interest in the other person. You need to keep confidences, share confidences of your own when appropriate, and simply demonstrate that you are on their side.
- Be able to have conversations that are very challenging and very supportive at the same time. If you have built up trust, you will be able to be very challenging, because your mentee will know that you have their best interests at heart.
- Not care about showing how much you know or how good you are – you should only care about asking the questions, giving the advice and feedback that will help your mentee.

- Be willing to get some training and coaching (even if you are
  already well on the way with the desire and raw talent), so that
  you can develop your mentoring skills to an excellent standard.

But if mentoring is not one of your strengths, be honest about it and make sure your people have mentors who really want to do it and are good at it. A good manager knows he or she is not perfect at everything and enlists other people to fill their gaps.

2. Give them regular feedback

Gen Y have been brought up by parents who regularly tell them how they are doing and give them ongoing feedback. This is positive as well as negative. The key, though, is that the *intention* behind the feedback is to help them to learn. Often managers fall into the trap of working themselves up to feedback only if they have a criticism to make of someone. No wonder that we tend to see feedback as judgemental rather than helpful.

Some managers also find it difficult to give positive feedback. Somehow they find it embarrassing and unnecessary.

The ability to give regular feedback (positive as well as negative) is an essential management skill. It always has been, but it is even more essential now that Gen Y have entered the workplace and expect and demand it. Receiving regular feedback is important to Gen Y. They want to learn from it. Give the feedback as often as you can. And if you feel like you need a little bit of help with your feedback skills or confidence, get hold of a coach or go on a short training programme. It will be worth the investment.

Rookie Buster

Receiving regular feedback is important to Gen Y. They want to learn from it.

The basics of giving feedback

- Have the right intention (that is, to help the person to realize what they are doing that is so good, or what they need to stop, and why).
- Always give a reason or rationale for the feedback.
- Give the feedback when you observe the behaviour. "Thanks, that information is exactly what I need for my report," is of much more use to the person than telling them three months later at their performance review when they probably won't remember what information they gave you.
- It doesn't have to be a long conversation. Giving the feedback followed by a "Well done" is all it takes.
- If you are telling someone something that they didn't do very well, do it in private, make sure you are specific, tell them as soon as possible, tell them why you are giving them the feedback, and ask if they need any help.
- If you find giving feedback difficult or uncomfortable, remember that by doing so you are (a) giving the Gen Y what they want, (b) giving them an opportunity to learn, and (c) improving performance.
- Get some practice – either with a coach or on a training course. The more you practise, the more skilled and confident you will become.

Finally, and crucially, make sure you focus on their strengths. Many managers spend far too much time trying to correct small weaknesses. Great performance comes when a person is playing to their strengths – it is more motivating too. Avoid trying to put square pegs into round holes as much as possible, and you won't go far wrong.

3. Explain the rationale behind decisions

No one likes being told what to do, or being told of a decision without understanding the reasons behind it. Many managers do this, though. It creates resentment amongst their people, who will not give genuine support and buy in unless they understand the reasons why. All generations get annoyed about this, but Gen Y will speak up.

Ideally you will ask the people who can contribute to do so anyway. And invite others to contribute and ask questions before the final decision is made. If it is a decision that, for some reason, has to be taken by a small group of people or senior management, test it out before you finalize it. And when you communicate more widely, be ready to face questions and give honest answers (even if the answer is "We hadn't thought of that"!).

Consider using collaborative technologies to solve problems, create policies and make decisions. One media company set up a wiki to create a policy on Facebook usage – there was a wide range of opposing views and lots of discussion. When it got heated, a moderator stepped in with helpful questions. After a couple of weeks a policy had been created. It was sensible and appropriate, because a whole range of people had contributed and so outlying opinions were heard and taken into account. And when it was communicated to the wider organization, everyone accepted it without question because they had all had a chance to participate and, even if they hadn't taken up that opportunity, they knew that lots of others had.

4. Manage the outcome, not the process

Gen Y work in a very different way to their older colleagues. It's a way that can appear to be chaotic and random when seen through the eyes of an X-er or Boomer. Technology is at the core of understanding why this is.

The way each generation organizes themselves is different, because they were conditioned in different technological contexts. If a Gen Y has arranged an outing to the cinema with friends, typically they will

78 agree an approximate time and place. But that can change many times in the hours and minutes preceding the meeting. They text and instant message each other, changing plans as they bump into others, have a better suggestion or change their mind. They *coordinate* their activities rather than plan them.

Their Boomer and Gen X colleagues have been brought up in a world where you make a plan and stick to it, not least because you could not instantly contact someone else with a last-minute change. They tend to stick to the commitments they make and avoid changing or letting people down at the last minute. Their style is more about *planning* than *coordinating*.

Neither approach is better than the other. But they do necessitate different management styles. When managing Gen Y it is much more effective to manage the outcomes, not the process (it could drive you wild if you even attempt to manage the process, as it may well seem far too disorganized!). This means that as a manager you need to be an enabler, not a checker. Make sure you are all agreed as to the goal or purpose of the project, then let them get on with it, and give them support and help as they go along if they need it. But don't check up on them frequently as you might have done if you were following a planned, project management approach.

Rookie Buster

When managing Gen Y it is much more effective to manage the outcomes, not the process. This means that as a manager you need to be an enabler, not a checker.

Similarly, in order to make their Boomer and Gen X colleagues feel comfortable, Gen Y may need to learn to work in a "planned" way from time to time, and may need some help and coaching with this.

Coach's notes

The essentials of managing Gen Y

1. Don't judge them on their behaviour (which will invariably be different from the behaviour you are used to and expect). Judge them on their intention – that means asking them about why they have done/are doing things as they are. Nine times out of ten "inappropriate" or puzzling behaviour is only inappropriate or puzzling because you don't see the world through their eyes and have not been conditioned in the way that they have.

2. Take time to explain to Gen Y why their older colleagues approach things as they do, and what the key differences are between generations.

3. Reinforce the message to all generations that you value the knowledge and strengths of them all. Otherwise you risk giving the impression that one way is the best way, when in fact a mixed generation team is a huge asset because of the different perspectives they bring.

4. Give regular feedback on how they are doing, remembering that they want to constantly learn. They will value having a formal performance review, but don't wait for that to come around before you give them feedback.

5. Become a mentor as well as a manager. Gen Y want to learn and want someone to learn from and receive feedback from. If mentoring is not your strength, help the Gen Ys in your team to find other mentors in the organization. It will pay huge dividends.

6. Always be ready to explain the rationale behind your decisions – Gen Y expect it, and they will question you when they don't understand.

Go for it! As the great management guru Peter Drucker has said: "In a knowledge economy there are no such things as conscripts – there are only volunteers. The trouble is, we have trained our managers to manage conscripts."

The key to managing Gen Y is to manage them as though they are volunteers. Give them lots of mentoring, feedback (they want to know how they are doing – good and bad), challenge and support, and you will have an energized, motivated and productive team who will exceed your expectations time and time again.

Notes

"How do I train and develop Generation Y?" is a question managers and HR people frequently ask. In relation to Gen Y, this is the wrong question. Sure, Gen Y do want their managers to support them and help them learn. The problem comes because each generation defines learning, training and development differently.

The clue to really effective development of Gen Y is in the title of this chapter. It is not about doing something to them, it's about providing opportunities for them to learn.

In this chapter you will learn how Gen Y learns and find tips for designing learning that works for them. Just as importantly, you will learn *why* they learn as they do and how their learning style differs from that of the other generations. This background understanding is vital if you are to make sure that all of the generations can learn effectively at work.

CHAPTER 6

How to develop Gen Y (or how to help them learn)

The essentials – what you need to know to understand how Gen Y learns

What has shaped how they learn?

Technology (of course) has been the big shaper of how Gen Y learns. There are other factors at play too, like the so-called "helicopter" parenting that they have experienced. Have a look into their world – it will shed light on why they are as they are:

- Instant access to information, facts and knowledge via Google and websites such as Wikipedia.
- Previous generations used to have to go to the library or ask someone; Gen Y just Google.
- Learning and reciting facts by rote is not important in a world where knowledge is available at our fingertips wherever we are.
- They use different places for different types of learning. They will study quietly and alone in libraries, and use that quiet reflection

84   time. They will also huddle around laptops with other students and learn collaboratively.

- The teacher is not the "expert", but a resource to help them learn.
- Learning together is not cheating.
- They are used to getting frequent feedback and attention from parents.
- Schools sometimes struggle to keep up with Gen Y's learning needs, because they are used to a world where they can customize what they want (such as iTunes, or their trainers) and get information when and where they need it.
- They grew up in a world of the internet and bite-sized information that comes at them as quickly as they can click a mouse. So more complex concepts or problems that cannot be instantly understood can be a challenge to Gen Y's patience.
- They are used to multi-tasking – there is a clear upside to that. The downside, though, is that they can sometimes have a short attention span. However, they have long attention spans if they are interested in what they are doing. It is all about relevance – if they feel something is worthwhile, they will stick at it. If not, they will switch off or start multi-tasking. One of my Gen Y mentees told me that when he is on training courses that he loses interest in, he starts making notes on other things or using his BlackBerry under the table.
- They grew up in a world where there is less reliance on experts who have a monopoly on knowledge (and therefore power). Doctors, teachers, lawyers – they can all be challenged much more easily now that lots of information is available on the web.

Differences in learning styles and preferences between the different generations

Good learning theory applies to development of all generations, of course, but there are some specific differences in each generation's preferences. These are worth knowing about, as they will influence the design of learning and training programmes. For example, if Boomers and Gen X don't believe that their trainer is an expert with relevant credentials and background, they will not have confidence in him or her. For Gen Y, the information and insight they are gaining from the trainer is more important than whether that person is a recognized "expert" or not.

Rookie Buster

For Gen Y, the information and insight they are gaining from the trainer is more important than whether that person is a recognized "expert" or not.

Below are the key differences between the generations. These differences make it a challenge to design learning events that are suitable for all generations, but it is still possible to achieve a blend of content and style to meet all their needs. And of course it will be useful to point out each group's differences, as it will enhance everyone's understanding and appreciation of their colleagues.

	Style	**Content**	**Delivery**
Boomers	Make me think, give me something new, convince me. Don't make me take part in role plays.	Has to be convincing, intelligent.	Has to be delivered by an authority on the subject. Lecture style is fine.

86

	Style	**Content**	**Delivery**
Gen X	Make it relevant and practical. Give me team exercises, in-tray exercises and role plays.	Has to be rigorous and relevant.	Has to be delivered by an expert. Involve me; make it interactive.
Gen Y	Make it relevant, practical and fun. Exercises are important, but make sure they are interesting.	Has to be applicable to my immediate needs.	Has to be engaging and two-way; take me on a journey.

What is Gen Y's preferred way of learning?

Understanding the context within which Gen Y grew up helps you to understand how they learn. It also helps you to understand why their learning preferences are so different from those of their older colleagues. Here, in a nutshell, are the important ingredients of learning the Gen Y way.

On-demand/instant responses
- They are used to Google and to being able to access information wherever they are, whenever they want to.
- They will seek the information they need from inside or outside their organization. For them, inside/outside are artificial barriers – they will go to where they think they are most likely to get the information.

- Technology has accustomed them to getting answers quickly – they can search YouTube and find a two-minute video that will tell them what they need to know, when they need to know it.

Constant feedback

- They are used to parents who are closely involved with their day-to-day activities and give them ongoing feedback as to how they are doing.
- Their use of technology has conditioned them into expecting not to have to wait for a response.
- Learning is a constant state, and so they look for the opportunity to learn in any situation – and the more feedback they can get, the better, because that's central to their ability to learn.

Learning with others

- They are used to playing computer games with people all around the world – some they know, some they don't. And they are used to helping one another with their homework, live and online. One teacher learned that some of her class were collaborating online to do their homework. Instead of making them wait until the next day at school to help them with anything they were stuck on, she got online herself so that she could be immediately available when they needed her.
- Doing homework together would have been tantamount to cheating for some older people. But to Gen Y it is not cheating, it is simply working together. The dominant school system of testing people mainly as individuals has not kept pace with the times.

Fast pace

- Again, because of technology, Gen Y is used to finding and consuming information very quickly. They use the internet and can "click-on" and "click-off" websites fast.
- They have a low tolerance to training sessions in which they are "talked at" for too long or subjected to too much PowerPoint.

88

The right medium

- It is a fallacy that Gen Y's preferred medium for learning is online. Sure, they are happy to learn from the web and from others via internet technology, but they are also keen to learn face-to-face from people.
- The main priority for Gen Y is that they *are* learning, not *how* they are learning. They will use the most appropriate method at the time.

Style

- Ideally, learning should be fun and entertaining. They have a low boredom threshold if they think something is not to relevant to them.
- They like to have a mix of auditory, visual and kinaesthetic aids to learning. They are after all used to multi-sensory computer games, including kinaesthetic ones (popularized by the Wii).

The environment

- It is important to remember that for Gen Y, learning is not associated with a place: learning is something they can do wherever they are.
- However, if you are organizing a specific learning event or training course, it is very important to pay attention to the physical environment. An inspiring physical environment helps all generations to learn. But while Gen X and Boomers are used to soulless training rooms, Gen Y aren't: they expect something uplifting, somewhere they want to be, somewhere that makes them feel good and so is conducive to learning.

Learning from many situations

- Gen Y are very keen to learn, and they look for learning in many situations. Their older

colleagues tend to think of learning as an event – a training course or mentoring conversation, perhaps – whereas Gen Y see learning potential in everything.
- Mentors can help Gen Ys to learn. They have so much information and data at their fingertips that mentors can also serve a useful purpose in helping them to sift out the useful information and discriminate between good-quality and bad-quality information.

Relevance
- In this information-rich world, Gen Y are used to quickly sifting to find what is relevant to them. They are used to being delivered relevant information at the press of a button. They are not interested in attending training courses or following e-learning packages that contain information that is not relevant (or that they don't think is relevant).
- They are used to being able to search for exactly what they want on websites such as YouTube – and to finding the information that they need when they need it.
- To keep their attention and keep them engaged, you need to make sure they understand the relevance of what they are learning.

Facilitators
- Old-style trainers just don't cut it with Gen Y. By "old-style", I mean the "chalk and talk" type – the ones who are there as experts to deliver knowledge. There is nothing wrong with experts, but they need to engage their students in a dialogue – as all the best educators have always done.
- Make sure your facilitators understand generational differences in learning styles, so that they can appeal to all generations in their classes.
- When hiring facilitators, ask them what they see their job as – you are looking for learning guides, not teachers.

Gen Y will always find ways to learn, whether you help them or not. It's just the way they are. A powerful way of making sure they learn as much as possible and remain engaged is to have them work with a skilled mentor. This doesn't have to be time consuming, but it is invaluable for them to have someone whom they can see or call regularly, for short bursts, to process what they are experiencing and learning.

Rookie Buster

Gen Y will always find ways to learn, whether you help them or not. It's just the way they are.

Given all this, it is easy to see why Gen Ys might be disillusioned with the development currently on offer in many organizations – which typically doesn't match their preferences. Most organizations offer a variety of training programmes and learning experiences (such as coaching and mentoring), but they don't necessarily treat learning as an ongoing process, nor do they think very much about what Gen Y need to learn and how best they learn.

Here are some simple ways to develop your Gen Ys and bring out the best in them.

What Gen Ys need to learn

Gen Ys of course need to learn what all young people have needed to learn when they enter the workplace – how the organization works, what it does, what its purpose is, and so on. But there are also other issues that Gen Y are finding they need to learn about at work. Their lack of understanding of these issues can cause inter-generational conflict at work, and this conflict is more pronounced now than it has been with other generations because of Gen Y's different values and attitudes (which we have already explored in previous chapters).

Here is what you may need to help Gen Y to understand:

- The other generations' differences, and why they are different.
- How to influence the other generations effectively.
- How to navigate organizational politics.

Gen Y need to understand that the other generations are different from them. They have different values and attitudes when it comes to work. At times they may feel that the other generations are being too rigid or controlling. If they understand why they are as they are, and what has shaped their behaviour, they will be able to influence them much more effectively, and inter-generational conflict will reduce.

Eight easy ways to develop Gen Y (and the other generations will appreciate them too)

1. **Get the induction right** – you would be surprised how many companies hand over a folder to new recruits, parade a number of senior managers in front of them to spout company messages, and talk "at" them about the company. First of all, they may well want to know things that are different from what you want to tell them. You have to offer more than just a question and answer session. Facilitate a dialogue, allow them to contact existing employees before they start their job, and allow them a chat facility to help get their questions answered in the first few weeks of employment.
2. **Make sure they have a good mentor** who can help them to learn. Even if this is the only development support you give them, provided they have a committed and well-trained mentor, it will have a powerful effect.
3. **Keep any training programmes focused and short** and make sure they are light on "input" and heavy on "discovery".
4. **Use technology where possible and appropriate** so that they can access the learning when they need it. For example, short YouTube-style videos showing someone how to use a piece of equipment, tips for how to handle a difficult conversation, and so

92 on. This way, they can search for the clips when they need them, whereas if they had learned them on a training course some time before, the chances are that they will have forgotten a lot of it by the time they need it.

5. **Make training participative** – Gen Y expect two-way dialogue. Whereas Gen X and Boomers want and expect "experts", Gen Y want facilitators.

6. **Provide them with the technology to learn collaboratively.** Give them the technology to build forums and discussion groups around particular topics. Also use wikis as a way of building and sharing knowledge. And messaging is a must – they need to be able to send short messages to seek help in order to learn as they go along.

7. **Make sure they understand the big picture** and can see the purpose in the learning. They need to understand it and know how they can influence it (whereas the other generations appreciated knowing how they fitted in, but didn't really expect to be told).

8. **Offer a variety of opportunities for Gen Y to learn.** Possibilities include job rotations, job swaps (outside the organization too – perhaps with client organizations) and involvement with projects that interest them inside and outside work.

To Gen Ys, learning is a participative process, not a process of simply receiving wisdom from experts. They do want to learn from experts – but not exclusively.

Rookie Buster

To Gen Ys, learning is a participative process, not a process of simply receiving wisdom from experts. They do want to learn from experts – but not exclusively.

Coach's notes

Here is your checklist for designing learning for Gen Y:

1. Keep it relevant.
2. See learning as an ongoing, constant activity rather a one-off.
3. Guide them to learn (a mentor is a great way of doing this) rather than having someone teach them.
4. Make it participative, fast paced and fun.
5. Provide opportunities to learn on-demand as much as possible.
6. Give them ongoing feedback – that is probably the most powerful tool in your armoury.

Go for it! Much of the guidance contained in this chapter is good practice in learning and development. It applies to all generations. The major difference when it comes to Generation Y is the technology – because they are used to using technology as a tool for learning. And, just as importantly, the learning behaviours driven by that technology are collaboration and sharing.

Understanding these generational differences is vital to providing effective development for Gen Y. As you will know from reading this chapter, there are simple tweaks and nuances that you can apply to your current development processes that will not only help Gen Y learn very effectively, but will increase their engagement levels too.

Notes

This chapter is important, because it is so easy to make wrong assumptions about (a) what someone from a particular generation means by a career, and (b) what they want from their career. The metaphor of the "career ladder" is central to many organizations' approach to career development. The notion that career progression is all about climbing a ladder still has some validity, but has some fundamental flaws when it comes to Gen Y and their view of career development.

If you are an employer and don't understand what "career development" means to Gen Y, you will certainly damage your ability to entice them into joining your organization and developing their career with you.

CHAPTER 7

Career development and Gen Y

What does "career development" mean to the different generations?

If you are in any way involved with helping Gen Y in their careers, then this chapter is a must-read for you. It will help you understand:

- What "career development" means to Gen Y (and how this differs from what it means to the other generations).
- How you can best support Gen Y in their career development.

It is important to look at what we mean by career. In the twentieth century, the term "career" usually referred to the work a person did to earn their money. It was particularly used in relation to people in the "professions" – for example, doctors, lawyers and architects.

Boomers and to some degree Gen X would generally make a career choice and start on a particular career path early on in their life, and stick to that path.

The notion that organizations are the places to develop your career was certainly true for the older generations, but is much less so for Gen Y.

98

	Boomers	**Gen X**	**Gen Y**
Their career "history"	Invariably the career that they remained in was the one they chose (or fell into) when they finished their formal education.	They will usually have chosen a particular career path. They may have changed part-way through, but generally Gen X stick to one career.	They will follow their interests, and if they decide to do something different after a while they won't see it as damaging to their career.
Where does career development take place?	They see the organization as the place to develop a career. Quite often that would be one organization where they would have had a "job for life".	Mainly in the organizational setting – but could be more than one. They would probably stay in any one job for at least three or four years before moving, typically "for promotion".	They see their career developing in a number of organizations and/or in self employment and voluntary work.

	Boomers	**Gen X**	**Gen Y**	99
Who's responsible?	Responsibility for their career development lies in large part with their employer.	They would say that they are responsible, but that it is incumbent upon their employer to present them with the opportunities to progress their career.	They believe that they are responsible, but the "deal" they do with their employer is that they develop in certain ways in return for selling their time to that particular employer.	
What does "getting on" mean?	Promotion, increased status, power, influence, money and responsibility.	Promotion, increased status, power, influence, money, responsibility and recognition.	Learning and growing in the areas they are interested in; opportunities to work with and learn from a whole range of people and situations. Promotion, increased status, power, influence, money, responsibility and recognition.	
What metaphor do they use?	A ladder.	A ladder.	A journey.	

Of course it would be wrong to generalize about what each generation defines as "getting on". Each generation values many of the same

100   things in their career that the other generations do: what is different is the relative importance of these things. Also, Gen Y value, want and expect the opportunity to learn and be fulfilled in their careers, whereas the other generations were conditioned to expect a "living" from work, but without expecting personal fulfilment. Boomers and X-ers are more concerned with what you might call the "hygiene" factors, or those things that are important for survival – money, securing your position (through power and influence) and gaining recognition from others, which is where status, job title and the like come in. Gen Y on the other hand still want the hygiene factors to be in place (although they seem to care less about status, except when it can bring them positive influence), but they are more interested in self development and are more self-referenced (in other words, it is more important that they themselves think they are getting on than that a senior boss tells them they are). That is not to say they don't want recognition – they like it. But they don't rely it as the only measure of how they are doing.

Rookie Buster

Gen Y value, want and expect the opportunity to learn and be fulfilled in their careers.

The way organizations approach career development is clearly more influenced by the Boomer and Gen X view of careers than it is by the Gen Y view. That is not surprising, of course, as the notion of what a career means has not changed much over many years, and the people who are responsible for employees' career development in most organizations are from the older generations themselves.

What you need to know about Gen Y and how they see their careers

The most important thing to remember is that each person is an individual, and so you need to understand what is important to that individual. Organizations do of course have to handle career development for many people – sometimes thousands of people – so it can be a challenge to take account of each individual's aspirations. It is possible to do this in a very manageable way, however. We will come back to this later.

Rookie Buster

The most important thing to remember is that each person is an individual, and so you need to understand what is important to that individual.

Having said that, there are common themes that emerge from the research and my work with hundreds of Gen Ys.

We heard Lamorna's story in Chapter 3. Let's take a look at what career development means to her and what she says she wants and expects from her career:

- "A chance to do interesting work and prove myself."
- "Work that means something to me and hopefully does some good for others."
- "Something that plays to my strengths and passions."
- "A challenge."
- "A chance to learn from my peers and from my mentors (of all ages)."
- "A work environment without barriers where I have a chance to be creative and rise to the challenge."

102 Lamorna earns a very modest salary and says that she would like to earn more to be able to pursue hobbies and interests, but that she would never take a job for the money if it didn't meet the criteria above.

Having had the experience of applying for and being rejected for many graduate schemes, she has come to the conclusion that there is no way she would fit into a typical organization – she says there are too many barriers.

The example of Lamorna is of course just one person's story, but there are lessons in it for those who are responsible for career development in organizations everywhere.

What career development opportunities do you need to offer Gen Y?

Here is what Gen Y want (but remember, this will vary from person to person – we will look at how to handle these varying needs later on in this chapter):

- **Meaningful work** – that is, work that is meaningful to them. Of course what is meaningful to one person may not be meaningful to another. The key is to find out what their work means to them – it may be about contributing to the community, it may be a chance to learn from others, to contribute to projects that they find exciting, to fight for justice… The list is endless, which is why it is important to understand what represents meaning to them. It is so easy to make incorrect assumptions when we hear the phrase "meaningful work".

- **A chance to do interesting work**, or work that they love. Again this varies from individual to individual. What is interesting work to one person may be deadly boring to another. There will be some people who love working on numbers and spreadsheets and solving numerical problems, while others would hate that. One of the traps we fall into as human beings is to assume that others are similar to us, and that what we find boring others also find boring. That is of course untrue. So, again the key is to find out what they love and what they find interesting. Regardless of the range of jobs you have to fill in your organization, each one of them will be interesting to someone out there.

- **The opportunity to learn**. As we have already seen in the previous chapter, this is a biggie for Gen Y. They see their careers much more in terms of the knowledge, skills and capabilities that they are able to pick up along the way, rather than as a set of steps up a promotional ladder (which is of course implicitly linked to a person's knowledge, skills and capability acquisition – but Gen Y care less about the ladder and more about the learning). Again, different people will be interested in learning different things. But learning is key. And ideally they will be given help in the form of training, development, coaching and mentoring. They like a challenge, and learning provides that challenge.
- **The opportunity to work with great people**. Time and time again, Gen Ys talk about the importance of colleagues. They want to work with people who are inspired and inspiring, and who are interesting and interested. This is partly linked to their desire to learn, and partly to their need to be part of a team of purposeful people.
- **Recognition**. Like the rest of us, Gen Y like recognition. They appreciate feedback and use the feedback to gauge how well they are progressing in their work and their career.
- **Promotion**. This is important to Gen Y for the recognition it implies and the increased influence that it brings. Some are interested in status, but even if status is important, it is of secondary importance. The problem is that many organizations get very wrapped up in the idea that to offer decent and appealing

career progression they have to be able to offer promotion (it's the ladder metaphor again). Promotion certainly plays a part (although not for all people), but there are many other aspects that are equally if not more important. And in this world of flattening organizational structures, the other elements are easier things to offer than promotion – which is limited, as there are only a certain number of positions on offer and they get fewer as you go up the ladder.

- "Show me the treat." This is the phrase one Gen Y used when he was asked what career development meant to him. He said he always wanted to know what "reward" was on offer for the efforts he made. In his particular case, the rewards he was interested in were primarily training and learning. He equated career progression with the acquisition of skills and knowledge and was keen to take up any learning opportunity that was given to him. He gave examples of learning opportunities he had had that he considered to be excellent career development. He had instigated most of them himself, and his company had supported him. Some of them were directly related to his job as a sales manager; others were not. They included: attending a day's seminar on Generation Y and technology (he got to attend for free in return for being on a Gen Y panel); a chance to devise a sales commission scheme with some guidance from a colleague; designing and developing a training manual for a call centre (this was a self-appointed task); and a management training course. All of these activities were his "treats". They kept him motivated and engaged because he felt he was developing his career, as well as learning how to do his job better.

Rookie Buster

There is a whole range of offerings you could give to Gen Y that would represent career development for them.

There is a whole range of offerings you could give to Gen Y that 105 would represent career development for them. You may not have thought of some of them as career development, but they may be very cheap and easy to offer. You are happy; the Gen Y is happy!

The practicalities – how to implement a career progression scheme that works for Gen Y

OK, so now you understand how Gen Y differ from their Gen X and Boomer colleagues. And you realize that it is impossible to generalize, as all of us see career development and progression in different ways. Given all of that, what can you do to provide a career development/ progression scheme that works for Gen Y?

Here are the three steps to an effective career development scheme.

1. Speak to them as early as possible

Ideally speak to them during the selection process about what career development means to them. Here are some useful questions:

- "What is important to you in a career?" (Many people will not have thought about this – by asking them this question you will help them, as well as the organization, to understand how to engage and retain this person.)
- "What do you mean by 'xxx'?" (This is a follow-up question that ensures you understand what exactly their definition is of what they have just told you – it is important you don't use your own definition, which more likely than not will be different from theirs.)
- "What will need to happen for you to feel that you are developing your career as you want to?"
- "From everything you have said, what are the most important top three in terms of feeling your career is developing?"

106   The answers to these questions will help you to understand what you need to do for this person in order for them to feel they are getting good career development. If there are things they want that you can't offer, it is best to know about this and have a conversation about it as early as possible. Perhaps you can talk through how else they may be able to achieve the development that can't be offered by your organization – maybe through voluntary work, job swaps, and so on.

The other benefit of gaining this insight is that there may be career development opportunities you currently offer that no one is interested in. By understanding their interests, and targeting your support to those interests, you could save time and money on courses and other activities that are not appealing.

2. Review what you have in place under the banner of "career development"

Typically, organizations have a suite of training courses, mentoring schemes, a promotion ladder, job rotations and placements. Assess each of your current "offers" against what the Gen Ys have told you they want. It may be that some of them are not appealing, or it may be that some are misunderstood and simply need to be re-described in a way that "sells" the benefits in Gen Y's language. For example, a job placement scheme in a customer organization could be a very appealing prospect if you explain how much the participants will learn and extend their network of contacts.

3. Help the Gen Y to articulate a simple "career development" plan

The "career development" plan should contain the answers to all the questions in Step 1 and also contain some detail of how they will achieve those needs. This plan is something they can review frequently with their manager, mentor and/or the graduate development manager. It is a great way of encouraging them to regularly reflect on how they are progressing. This is really important: often people are actually learning and developing on a day-to-day basis in all sorts of situations, but they don't think about the fact that this is developmental activity. Simply having good quality conversations about their development is very beneficial, and should be an intrinsic part of any career development strategy.

A core part of any career progression strategy is to:

(a) help the person to articulate what career development means to them;

(b) help them to identify what they can do to develop in the ways they want;

(c) pinpoint specifically how the organization can support them;

and, last but not least,

(d) have regular conversations about what they are learning and how that learning supports their career development.

Coach's notes

1. Understand (and challenge where necessary) the organization's assumptions about what career development/ progression means.
2. Build into your recruitment and induction process a conversation with each new hire that elicits their career development aspirations.
3. Appoint one person to be responsible for having ongoing, regular conversations with your Gen Ys about their development and how what they are doing contributes to their stated career progression goals.
4. Make sure that the person with whom they have the ongoing development conversations is skilled at handling good conversations.
5. If you involve them in some career development activity that the organization has identified as important, help them to understand why. Explain the benefits to them as well as to the organization.
6. If any of your people have career development aspirations that cannot be achieved in your organization, then be honest about that and explain why. Gen Y don't expect you to deliver everything they want, but they expect openness and transparency.

Go for it! Remember Lamorna? She had a clear idea of what career development meant to her. She didn't expect anyone to deliver it on a plate; she just expected them to be interested in what she wanted to achieve and to support her as much as possible. Many organizations get bogged down in elaborate career development processes and programmes and lose sight of the basics. They also get very worried about being able to "manage people's expectations", when in reality they do not have a good understanding of those expectations to start with. It should be clear from this chapter that good quality, regular conversations are at the core of a great career development scheme.

Get the basics right and you will not go far wrong. You will have a workforce of people who feel listened to, understood and supported. And where you cannot support them in their career aspirations, they will understand why. This of course applies not just to Gen Y, but to all generations, and it will lead to an engaged group of productive people who appreciate and feel loyal to their organization.

Teamwork has always been a challenge for organizations. When teams work well they can move mountains. When there are problems in a team, they can seriously inhibit its ability to be productive and creative.

Anyone who has worked in a team will understand that the dynamics of a team can be complex at the best of times. Add to that the different attitudes and values of each generation, and, as we have seen in previous chapters, the potential for misunderstanding is high. But so is the potential for truly innovative and effective working, for the simple reason that without diversity, innovation is not possible.

CHAPTER 8

How do you build effective cross-generational teams?

What cross-generational teams can do

Innovation relies on a number of different and divergent perspectives being brought to bear on a problem. A mixed-generation team inevitably contains a diversity of perspectives and views which, if channelled well, leads to the best solutions, the best products and a highly engaged team.

Get it wrong, and it can mean conflict, ineffective working and a feeling of frustration for the team members.

Get it right, and you can release knowledge, wisdom and talent from all generations. A great cross-generational team feels vibrant, and there is a sense of learning and fun within and between the generations.

Rookie Buster

A great cross-generational team feels vibrant, and there is a sense of learning and fun within and between the generations.

112   Before we go any further on the subject of cross-generational teams, let's just pause for a minute and look at what we mean by teams. Essentially, for this purpose there are three types of team:

1. Those whose team is the organization or department/group they work in. These can obviously be large teams with a common overall purpose but little day-to-day contact or experience of working together.
2. The smaller groups that people work in and with which they share some specific common goals – for example, an HR department.
3. The project team – that is, a group of people who have come together for a particular period of time to achieve a specific goal.

Clearly in today's world that is not an entirely accurate representation of the concept of teams. People who haven't met can collaborate online to develop open source technology, for example. Loose networks of people can communicate and sometimes work together towards a common purpose. Work boundaries are becoming increasingly blurred. The purpose of this chapter is not to try and address all possible definitions and configurations of the term "team", but to help you to understand the ways in which different generations work together, and how to help them to work productively across generation boundaries.

Inevitably most teams today are made up of two or more different generations, so understanding how to have them work really well together is important. This chapter will give you the insight and practical guidance you need to build excellent and productive cross-generational teams.

How do the different generations work in teams?

Each generation has a different style of working in a team. Let's take a look at the different team styles and preferences of the different generations. It is important for everyone to understand these if they are to

work together in a productive way, not in order to stereotype the dif-   113
ferent generations, but in order to understand where they are coming
from and how they work together in teams.

	Boomers	**Gen X**	**Gen Y**
Teamworking style	Teamwork is about "pulling together" and "team spirit". Team meetings are scheduled at key points in the project (a planned approach).	Value the unique contributions that people can make. Team meetings are scheduled at key points in the project (a planned approach).	Trust and openness is paramount. Want team meetings only when they are needed – little and often.
Their values/style in teams	Must have common purpose, values, goals, etc. It's important that people "fit".	Realize that diversity is good, but sometimes struggle with it. Like the networking aspects of teamworking.	Like to know the bigger picture and purpose. Diversity is exciting and challenging to them – it's an opportunity to learn. Status not an issue – they speak to the "person" not the "position".

114

	Boomers	**Gen X**	**Gen Y**
Preferred team-work medium	Face-to-face.	Prefer face-to-face; know that virtual contact is needed, but not that comfortable with it.	Like face-to-face and comfortable with virtual teamworking. Technology is an important tool for sharing (e.g. wikis) and communication "on-demand" (e.g. instant messaging).
Their concerns/ weaknesses	Tendency to defer to more senior team members may get in the way.	"Knowledge is power" – they may be reluctant to share. Individualistic and competitive tendencies may get in the way.	Can appear too "random" for Boomers and X-ers and may need to receive coaching on project planning and formal feedback mechanisms. Can appear to be disrespectful to more senior team members.

What are Gen Y like as team members?

The characteristics and behaviour of Gen Y in a team can bring huge benefits as well as conflict. Let's take a look at the Gen Y characteristics, with specific reference to teamwork. It depends upon 115 your perspective as to whether you judge these characteristics to be helpful or unhelpful in a team environment. To a large extent it depends upon what kind of culture you want to foster.

This list is not meant to be an exhaustive list of Gen Y's preferences and behaviours. It is meant to help you to understand the contribution Gen Y can make in a team and the possible implications of their team behaviour.

Gen Y characteristics	Implications
More likely to speak up, challenge and ask the uncomfortable questions.	Very useful in terms of pursuing the goals of the team, but may be very uncomfortable for others and can cause conflict.
Not deferential to authority and see all team members as "equal". They talk to "people" not "positions".	Again, can be uncomfortable for other people in the team, but it leads to much better quality conversations and ultimately better outcomes.
They respond to mentoring, not being told what to do.	This is great if the team develops a culture of co-mentoring. Can cause problems if team members step into an unhelpful "command and control" mode.
They are natural networkers and will involve people outside the team (and sometimes outside the organization).	This is clearly helpful in terms of bringing to bear a range or ideas and resources. The downside is that some members of the team may feel protective of the team and unwilling to loosen the boundaries of the team "wall".

116

Gen Y characteristics	Implications
Naturally optimistic and can come across as very confident.	These characteristics are on the whole very positive. However if optimism is overdone it can turn into lack of realistic expectations – and it can look like arrogance and annoy other team members.
They tend to multitask and organize their work in less of an obviously "planned" way than the other generations do.	Multi-tasking can be good when it means a person is being fast and efficient. The Gen Y preferred way of working can seem chaotic to others. The key is to focus on the outcomes, not the process.
They set great store by trust and good relationships in a team.	This may be seen by some as focusing on the relationships at the expense of the task in hand. But of course both are important.
They gravitate to doing only the work that they are particularly interested in and that gives them a buzz.	This is fine as long as all team members are able to choose the roles and tasks that they are interested in too. And if all team members' interests are being met it will make for a high-performing and energetic team.

You may be thinking that making teams of different generations work together is a nightmare. Well, it can be if you don't understand how each generation is different, and the simple steps you need to take to make the team work.

Also, and importantly – you need to be convinced it's worth it. So here are the benefits.

What are the benefits of effective cross-generational teams?

Most organizations today are, by definition, multi-generational groups of people. It follows therefore that most organizations would benefit from understanding how to get the most from their entire workforce and helping them to work productively together.

As with any diverse group of people working together, different generations working together can bring huge benefits to the individual, the group and the organization. The benefits listed below are as applicable to large teams (entire organizations) as they are to small project teams.

The specific benefits of effective cross-generational teams include:

- **Increased insight into different customer age segments.**
  Bringing a range of perspectives to bear on an issue is clearly important when working on issues that affect your customers and individual consumers, as it means that you are taking account of a range of ages/generations.
- **Improved knowledge sharing and knowledge management.**
  Organizations often struggle with how to capture and share the immense knowledge of the senior people in an organization. Mentoring is one way of doing this, as is good cross-generational team working. The informal networking aspects of a dynamic team are also a fantastic medium for surfacing the knowledge and wisdom of its members.
- **Breaking down hierarchical and status barriers.** These barriers can be unhelpful when they inhibit open conversations, sharing and healthy challenge. The more the different generations can understand about one another and work together, the more the barriers will be broken down.
- **Better solutions.** When people with diverse views and perspectives work together, provided they learn to listen to and work with this diversity, they inevitably produce better solutions and products than homogeneous teams can produce.

When setting up project teams, before getting stuck into the task in hand, spend time getting them to look at the benefits of working together and bringing different views and perspectives to bear. This signals that it is fine – in fact, desirable – to have different views and to disagree at times.

Rookie Buster

> It is fine – in fact, desirable – to have different views and to disagree at times.

So, on to the nitty gritty – how do you make a team work when you have a whole load of different preferences, characteristics and opinions, not to mention personality types, involved?

I'm not saying it's easy, but it is a whole lot easier than some people think. Follow these steps and you will be in good shape.

Seven steps to great teamwork

Step 1. Spend some time with the whole team exploring their generational and style preferences

Obviously if the whole team is a large group of people it is most effective to do this work in people's immediate work groups or project teams. Team leaders often introduce the use of personality preference tools, such at the Myers-Briggs Type Indicator questionnaire. Most people don't think to look at generational differences, but this is an area that organizations who really understand the value of diversity (of ideas, thoughts and perspectives) pay attention to. Use the table on pages 113–14 to start a discussion on differences and the benefits and disadvantages of different behaviours in a team. By having these discussions up front you create an atmosphere and a language for people to use when the going gets tough and disagreements occur.

It's important to say here that disagreement within teams is not a $\qquad$ 119
bad thing. It can on the contrary be a good thing, if it gives the team a
chance to work on and resolve their differences, leading to more productive relationships and outcomes. However, if conflict is not
managed well it can cause lasting damage to the team.

Rookie Buster

Disagreement within teams is not a bad thing. It can on
the contrary be a good thing, if it gives the team a chance
to work on and resolve their differences.

Step 2. Make sure the team's purpose is clear

It's not just Gen Y who like to understand the big picture and their part
in it. When the team first forms (and when new members join), spend
time exploring, agreeing and clarifying the purpose of the team and
everyone's part in it. Make sure that new employees' induction includes
spending time looking at the organization's and team's purposes as
well as their own purpose.

Step 3. Allow time for relationships to gel and trust to build

This cannot be forced, but it can
be facilitated. Spending time
exploring people's preferences
(Step 1) will help get this process
kick-started. And build in
plenty of time for the team to
spend with each other on both
work and non-work activi-
ties. As and when issues
come up that threaten to
damage trust in the team
(like when a conflict arises),

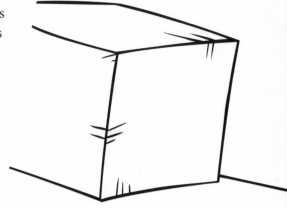

120   see it as an opportunity to deepen the trust rather than allowing it to damage relationships. Examining trust in teams is a whole book in itself, but essentially if you encourage the team to speak openly to each other and to air disagreements, this will build trust. If views and opinions are suppressed it will only result in team members "leaving the team" emotionally and/or encourage factions to develop.

Rookie Buster

> If you encourage the team to speak openly to each other and to air disagreements, this will build trust.

Step 4. Allow time to review how the team is doing

Many teams get so into the task in hand that they don't give any time or attention to the individuals, relationships or team dynamics. This doesn't have to be onerous. It can be as simple as having a short "check in" and "check out" at the beginning and end of team meetings and asking people the following questions:

- What is it like working in this team – what is working well and/or do any changes need to be made?
- As a team are we using each person's preferences to positive advantage or are the different preferences causing conflict?

Give each person a couple of minutes to answer each question and appoint someone as a facilitator of the session so that you stick to time and stay on the point. If any problems or concerns come up, give them airtime – this may feel to some like wasting time, but if you don't resolve any issues as quickly as possible they will waste a lot more in the long run.

Step 5. Don't focus exclusively on the task

A great team pays attention to the individuals in the team, their relationships and their levels of engagement. Regular quick reviews will allow airtime for all the non-task aspects of excellent teams. This process will build trust, improve communications and allow people to get to know one another and develop a great team spirit. Gen Y are used to collaborating and have grown up with the notion of communities. This is natural territory for them, and they will be much more engaged if due attention is given to all aspects of the team, not just the task in hand.

Step 6. Help them to learn

Efficiency and innovation only happen if people keep on learning. Gen Y is very hungry to learn and will expect to receive feedback, and will also expect others in the team to want to hear feedback from them. It is important to create an atmosphere in which this is welcomed. For most people, learning doesn't just magically happen: they need to be given the time and space to reflect, to be asked good questions and to be given quality feedback. This shouldn't be a weighty process. It's a five-minute "Hey, John, have you got a minute to review how that client meeting went so we can improve and build on it next time?" This approach will build a culture in which people question and give feedback with the intention of learning, growing and improving. Having at least a few role models – people who are skilled coaches and mentors – in the team is invaluable. If you haven't already got them, find a few people who are naturally talented and interested coaches and ask them to facilitate learning in the team whenever they have a chance.

Rookie Buster

Gen Y is very hungry to learn and will expect to receive feedback, and will also expect others in the team to want to hear feedback from them.

122 **Step 7. Talk honestly about failures and celebrate successes**

Open and honest communication in a team is crucial. People need to feel as though they can speak up. Gen Y are naturally inclined to do that anyway, so may be a good role model. Honest talking means being able to raise anything, good or bad, with the greater good of the team in mind. Celebrating successes is really important too. We all like the feeling of a job well done, and recognition, in its many forms, is important to most people. Celebrate success when it occurs, and recognize the contributions of everyone.

All of the seven steps are of course valid for any team. Teams that are made up of different generations (as well as different personality types) have a great possibility for success because of the diversity they bring, but they also have a great possibility for conflict for that same reason.

In a world that is changing so fast, the ability to engage people's talents to the maximum is what sets the great organizations apart from the mediocre ones. Creating excellent teamwork should be a priority, because not doing so will certainly damage your ability to create the ideas, products, services and relationships that all organizations need in order to be truly successful.

Great teamwork is a crucial source of competitive advantage. If you are not sure how to go about it, or think you could be doing better, bring in a coach or someone who can help you to do it. Your goal should be to develop a strong in-house capability in teamwork.

Rookie Buster

Great teamwork is a crucial source of competitive advantage.

Coach's notes

1. Run short workshops to show team members how to explore different generational and personality preferences and appreciate the value (and potential conflict) that comes from these differences.

2. Train managers and leaders to understand, manage and engage cross-generational teams.

3. Make sure that you have some team members (including the team leader) who have a passion for mentoring and coaching, and the skills to do it well. Ongoing learning is essential to productive teams, and coaches and mentors help people learn.

4. Use the seven steps to great teamwork, and encourage dialogue with the team about what great teams do.

5. Ask the team how they want to change or improve the way they work – make them responsible, but give them guidance and training to enable them to live up to the responsibility.

6. Encourage all team members to be responsible for effective teamwork. Do this not by "imposing" rules, but by discussing, training, coaching and, most importantly, encouraging two-way communication.

Go for it! Each generation has its own knowledge and wisdom. It is not true that older people are always the wiser ones, and that it is for them to teach the younger generations. All the generations can learn from each other. Each brings its own perspectives, wisdom, skills and gifts to a team.

If you create an atmosphere in which everyone plays to their strengths and rich cross-generational diversity is valued, you will have not only a vibrant, dynamic team, but also a competitive advantage.

Notes

This book is primarily aimed at those who want to understand how to attract, manage and engage Gen Y as employees. However, employees are also consumers, and consumers are also employees. As I discovered from my work in marketing and sales, there is a direct link between how we manage and work with our employees and whether that encourages them to help us to market and sell well or not. Smart companies use their Gen Y employees to help them to understand and sell to Gen Y consumers and customers.

CHAPTER 9

How to appeal to Gen Y consumers

Generation Y as a market

I first became aware of Generation Y as a market when I was working in the media industry for The Economist Group (publisher of *The Economist* newspaper). Marketing people and advertisers realized that this generation was quite different, in terms of their attitudes and values, from consumers of other ages. They started to take steps to understand Gen Y so that they could appeal to them.

The so-called "grey market" is very important to many organizations these days, because the population is ageing, and this age group often has more time and disposable income. But some organizations and sectors are either losing or not gaining young consumers at the rate they need to in order to sustain and grow their businesses. The media industry is exercising its brains about this as technology changes and consumers start to use media content in very different ways. The electronics products industry has transformed into the "digital entertainment" industry. Other industries are perhaps not yet taking such a radical look at their business models and product offerings as the media and the electronics industries have. But even if their products

128   do not need to change in the next few years, they will certainly have to look at the ways they communicate with and market and sell to their consumers and customers. To understand their Gen Y consumers (and those of other ages who have similar behaviours to Gen Y due to the technological changes), they will have to get a deep insight into their values, needs and preferences.

Gen Y is just a manifestation of a profound and fundamental technological change that is picking up pace in the world as more people get connected and more organizations adjust their business models. This is important to remember, because some people think that Gen Y are going to change and become more like Boomers and Gen X. They won't, because they have grown up in a very different technological paradigm that is driving some important changes in people's attitudes and behaviour.

Rookie Buster

Some people think that Gen Y are going to change and become more like Boomers and Gen X. They won't.

As we have seen, Gen Y are natives of the digital world; the rest of us are immigrants. They will always have more of an inherent, natural understanding of the digital world than we do because they have always used technology. Boomers and Gen X are digital immigrants – and just like people who learn a new language, they will always need to translate the new language into their own to a greater or lesser extent. We will take a closer look at this and its implications later.

In this chapter we are going to take a look inside the minds of Gen Y. You will learn about what makes them tick, and gain an understanding of how to appeal to, and do business with, your current and potential Gen Y consumer or customer base.

Rookie Buster

Generation Y are natives of the digital world; the rest of us are immigrants.

The essentials – what do you really need to understand about Gen Y?

The most important thing you need to understand is the context that Gen Y have grown up and been educated in. This understanding will give you an insight into their behaviour. When you visit a country whose culture is very different from your own, it is not enough to understand the local people's habits and manners. To really get an insight into what makes them tick, you need to understand the under-lying values that create the behaviour (or habits). If you don't, you will only have a shallow understanding and will not gain any insight into why people are as they are.

For example, you may well know that some people in the UK who are currently in their eighties tend not to buy premium food brands. If you are a marketer of premium food brands, you may try and find all sorts of ways to appeal to this group and entice them to buy. But you need insight into why they don't buy these brands. You may find that because World War II and food rationing were happening during their formative years, they believe that spending money on premium food brands is a waste of money. However, premium food brands are also very appealing to some people in that age group simply because those foods were not available when they were growing up.

In Chapter 1 we looked at the context in which Gen Y grew up in order to understand how that has shaped their behaviour.

As marketing people know only too well, human behaviour is a complex thing. It is difficult to define and predict. And it is important to understand your target market as much as you possibly can in order to avoid making dangerous assumptions about them. That said, here are some of the essentials that you need to know about Gen Y if you are to appeal to them and attract and keep hold of Gen Y consumers and customers:

- They have very good spin detectors. For a number of reasons, Gen Y are much less susceptible to spin than Boomers and Gen X are. They have witnessed the corporate scandals of the last decade and have seen the decline in trustworthiness of business people and politicians. They are used to a straightforward communication style, because internet usage means they are accustomed to clicking on and off websites to find what is relevant to them. Websites have just seconds to get their message across, so the copy on these sites is much more succinct and to the point. Gen Y want to know "what's in it for them" quickly. And they have low tolerance for overstated or false claims.

Rookie Buster

Gen Y are much less susceptible to spin than Boomers and Gen X are.

- Openness and honesty is important to them. They appreciate and demand honesty as much as they shun spin. One of the reasons why Obama got the young generation's vote was that he represented an openness and honesty that they had not seen in other politicians. He used Facebook to win them over, to appear accessible and to talk to them in their preferred medium. They have learned to trust people they don't know by doing business with them on websites such as eBay and Amazon. These sites operate on openness and trust. And that honesty is monitored and rated by the consumers themselves.
- They are quick to decide what is relevant to them and what is not. You don't have much time to grab their attention. They are used to having a stream of communications at their fingertips, so they are

accustomed to sifting out what is not applicable to them or does   131
not immediately interest them.

- They are used to having choice. There is a proliferation of websites
that compare products and services and help consumers to make
choices. Increasingly consumers do not have to buy standard
products. Having to accept "standard" products or services does
not make sense to Gen Y. Being accustomed to choice also means
that they expect excellent standards of customer service, because
those who provide high standards get their business – the
organizations who offer customization tend also to deliver great
customer service.

Rookie Buster

Having to accept "standard" products or services does
not make sense to Gen Y.

- They don't rely on experts. Gen Y has grown up in the Google
world. They are used to being able to search for the information
they need and to being able to track down people who may be
able to help them. So when they visit their doctor or
lawyer, they arrive armed with a lot of information
and probing questions. They do not take what
"experts" say at face value, as many Boomers
and Gen Xs had to. For them it was difficult to
find information – they did not have the
internet and so relied on a very small group of
people to tell them what they needed to know.
Gen Y's equivalent of experts are the users and
consumers whose blogs they read and trust, or
who they find in chat rooms discussing products,
service and organizations – basically it is possible
to find communications on every imaginable

132 subject. Gen Y know how to access this information and insight. And the views of your customers will be more interesting to them than the official information on your website. They may not even bother to visit your website.

- They are aware of and interested in ethical issues. This is a generation who will snub companies because of their allegedly exploitative labour practices. Because of the internet and their connections on social networking sites they are well informed about such issues. They actively look for and choose ethical products and service, and for many, being associated with them is an important part of their identity.

- They have grown up with the notion of social entrepreneurship. Since Gen Y has been aware of the world, there has emerged a whole new generation of social entrepreneurs. They know about Bill Gates's business empire, but they also know about his philanthropic values and work. There are many people in the public eye now who have successful careers and are pioneers of change and good. In the UK Jamie Oliver has staffed some of his restaurants with unemployed young people; the Eden Project is an inspiring example of social entrepreneurship by its founder Tim Smit; and *The Big Issue* is a newspaper sold by homeless people with the goal of helping them. Making a profit by doing good is a model that appeals to Gen Y. And their world is full of examples of that: eBay is ubiquitous now. Who would have thought it would have taken off? Many traditional business people wouldn't. Jeff Skoll, its founder, wanted to promote social values and business based on trust.

  There are plenty of other less well-known local social entrepreneurship projects. And many Gen Ys, even if they are not involved in such a project themselves, may well have peers who have opted to become social entrepreneurs.

Remember that generation is about attitude, not age. And whilst these characteristics are true of the Gen Y population, they will inevitably not be common to *all* Gen Ys. A proportion of Boomers and Gen X will also share some of Gen Y's characteristics. So it is important to

segment your population in terms not just of age, but also of 133
behaviour.

Common mistakes when marketing and selling to Gen Y

Without the above insight into Gen Y it is easy to get your marketing
and selling wrong. Some traps that organizations fall into are:

- Assuming Gen Y think the same way as Boomers and Gen X. And
  that the same things are important to them.
- Assuming they know what's important to this generation, and
  getting it wrong. For example, thinking that because Gen Y like
  technology they love to do everything online. They use the media
  that is appropriate at the time, but it is not always the internet.
- "Intruding" into Gen Y's spaces. For example, trying to sell to
  them on Facebook. It's not that they don't want to be sold to, but
  they want to be sold products that are relevant to them at a time
  of their choosing. This does not mean that you cannot venture on
  to Facebook, but if you do, go there only if you
  are sure that Gen Y will agree that what you
  have is genuinely interesting to them
  (you may think it is, but they may
  not!).
- Talking down to them. This
  generation is savvy and has got
  little time for being patronized.
  As we have already learned,
  they can see through spin and
  they know what they want.
  Unless you respect them and
  genuinely listen to them, they simply won't do
  business with you.
- Using blogs as sales tools. There have been
  well-publicized cases of companies setting

up blogs and having people promote their goods and services whilst hiding the fact that this person is writing on behalf of the company. In all cases this has backfired badly, because Gen Y do not tolerate being "tricked". When speaking to Gen Y, PR and marketing has to have complete integrity and be very honest. Of course they should treat the other generations like that too, but in the past have got away with not doing so.

Rookie Buster

This generation is savvy and has got little time for being patronized. Unless you respect them and genuinely listen to them, they simply won't do business with you.

In a nutshell, the most common mistakes fall into two categories: not understanding the Gen Y audience, and/or not being honest and straightforward with them. These are pretty much the same mistakes that you can make with any audience – but Gen Y are probably less forgiving!

How to appeal to and attract the attention of Gen Y

The secret to appealing to Gen Y is simple:
- Give them what they want and need; and
- Engage with them in ways they find interesting and compelling.

Sound easy? It is if you understand them. All you need is some decent insight and the right kind of creativity.

So, what do they find compelling? 135

- A cause. If you can rally Gen Y behind a genuine cause, they will love it. This doesn't just mean telling them how much of your profits you give to charity; it could include breaking down monopolies, creating more democratic means of doing business or just doing something good that appeals to people's sense of justice and fairness. An example from a few years ago was the launch of the American Express "Red" card. One per cent of the amount spent on the card is donated to something called the "Global Fund", which was created in 2002 to fight the spread of malaria, tuberculosis and AIDS. The U2 star and political activist Bono was active in the launch of the card, to lend even more credibility to its values.

- Something that directly meets their needs or is interesting or entertaining to them. This is really no different from appealing to any consumer group. These days you have to work harder to get what the ad agencies call "standout". An example of that was a campaign that Agency Republic ran for O2. The campaign was called "Favourite Place" and included a Facebook group where graduates and undergraduates voted for their favourite university. Scores were updated daily. There were prizes for those who voted and posted. The results were brand engagement that far exceeded O2's expectations. It was probably no coincidence that Agency Republic is a vibrant place full of Gen Y (or digital native) employees. This campaign hit the mark for the young consumers and probably ticked all three of the "interesting", "entertaining" and "something in it for me" boxes.

136
- Honest and straightforward language. It's not so much that they find honest and straightforward language compelling, but that they find the opposite a turn-off. It's a must-have. Ideally the writers you use will have a natural style that appeals to Gen Y. Trying to fake a "voice" that appeals to them is generally a road to disaster.
- Collaborate with them and co-create. The one-way supplier-consumer relationship is anathema to Gen Y. They expect more than focus groups to glean their opinion; they expect to be able to be involved in product development, they expect their opinions to count, and in some cases they expect to be able to co-create content too. An example of that is the National Trust, a UK conservation and heritage charity, whose members post photos on Flickr – a photo sharing website – of National Trust properties that they have visited. No one asks them to and they don't get paid for it, but they are so engaged with the National Trust that they do it because they want to. There are numerous websites such as Wikipedia and Facebook that use content created for them by their users. It is a new, democratic way of doing business that is second nature to Gen Y.

  Dell has been a leading light in customer collaboration. At DellIdeaStorm.com, a social website that the company launched in 2007, people are invited to make suggestions for products and services. Apparently they receive thousands of suggestions, a good number of which have been implemented.
- Give them great customer service. They absolutely expect it and take action if they don't get it. The story of Comcast, a communications company, tells you all you need to know on this topic. The company received plenty of bad publicity and its reputation was badly damaged when a video was posted on YouTube showing one of their technicians asleep on a customer's sofa whilst on hold to Comcast. And a website called www.comcastmustdie.com was set up. Subsequently one of Comcast's customers had a problem with his new high definition TV and posted a gripe about it on Twitter. Within minutes he had received a reply, and within hours a Comcast technician had

arrived to fix the problem. The company now encourages its employees to do what the person who responded to the Twitter comment did – browse social network sites and online forums so that as soon as problems are talked about they can be picked up and resolved.

And at Southwest Airlines, they employ a chief Twitter officer, who tracks Twitter comments and monitors a Facebook group and who interacts with and helps bloggers. So if someone posts a complaint in cyberspace, the company knows about it and can respond in a personal way.

You can't control the image your organization has in the market-place any more, if you ever could. There will be people saying good and bad things online, and word spreads much quicker than in the days before the internet. The best thing you can do is make sure you have people interacting with your customers online, helping them and picking up problems so that you can resolve any problems quickly. This relies on employing people who are comfortable in the online world and have excellent customer service values.

Rookie Buster

The best thing you can do is make sure you have people interacting with your customers online, helping them and picking up problems so that you can resolve any problems quickly.

Coach's notes

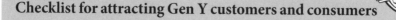

Checklist for attracting Gen Y customers and consumers

- Make sure you really understand them – get as much insight as you possibly can.
- Connect with them on their terms and in their language.
- Don't treat them in a transactional way – they want two-way communication and collaboration.
- Remember, you cannot control what they say about you – but make sure you find out by keeping abreast of where they hang out online. And respond to them quickly, helpfully and honestly.
- But the hottest tip of all is to employ great Gen Ys and engage them in helping you to figure out how to respond to their Gen Y consumers. This means getting them truly involved in strategy, sales, customer service, marketing and product development.

Go for it! Because of the hierarchical nature of most organizations, the people who make the important decisions in all these expert areas are Boomers and Gen Xs, simply because they are usually the most senior. But the companies who will really get ahead with Gen Y consumers and customers will be the ones who have Gen Ys themselves involved in shaping the future.

140

The previous chapters give advice and guidance on how to attract, engage and manage Gen Y, both as employees and as consumers. We have looked at organizational cultures, processes, how managers and leaders behave, and the HR, marketing and sales strategies we can use.

This chapter provides an overview of some of the things you can do to attract and keep the talent you need for success now and in the future. To become an organization that Gen Y flock to work for. Forget the war for talent. The best companies don't have to compete in a war for people; they have the best ones queuing up to work for them. In years to come, that will be essential. As the working population gets older, there will be a shortage of good people to keep global organizations and economies going. Think of this book as a handy manual to help you build the bridge from where you are now to being a future-proofed company.

Make your organization *so* appealing to Gen Y employees and customers/consumers that you will not have to worry about the global talent shortage. And make it so adaptable that you are able to positively exploit new ways of working and new technologies.

CHAPTER 10

The future – how you need to respond to the changing world of work

The context

Clearly we are in a time of big and fast technological change – some say, the biggest changes since the invention of the printing press in 1440. These technological changes mean that the world in general moves faster, as people are able to communicate faster and across geographical boundaries. The other crucial piece of context is the changing demographic situation.

Governments all over the world have been aware for a long time of the changes in population trends and the predictions that experts are making. For quite some time they have been looking into how the younger generation of workers are going to be able to sustain a growing aged population. In the UK the fastest growing age group is the over-80s. In Spain, Italy and Germany only around 15 per cent of the population is under age 15; 18 per cent is 65 and over. In China, Japan and South Korea the numbers of young people are falling, not only as a proportion of the total population but also in absolute numbers. In the USA only 20 per cent of the population is under age 15, and 13 per cent is aged 65 or over.

142   What does all this mean for you? Well, it means that no matter which countries you operate in, you will find that the number of new entrants to the workplace is lower. The best talent will be in high demand, and they will have choices. You will have to compete ever harder to attract them. The organizations that do well will be the ones that really understand the Gen Ys, and how to attract and keep them.

Rookie Buster

The organizations that do well will be the ones that really understand the Gen Ys, and how to attract and keep them.

If you haven't already got to grips with this issue, it is really important to do so now. Some organizations are finding that, regardless of the economic downturn which is happening at the time of writing, their difficulty in finding enough good people is inhibiting their business development.

Where to start?

Think about the importance of your people, and how you are harnessing the knowledge and skill of all generations in the workplace. Boomers and Gen X have a lot of knowledge and experience in all aspects of running businesses. Gen Y clearly have a deep understanding of new technologies, and therefore different ways of collaborating, learning and working. These people are employees and consumers and can help you figure out what products and services you need to offer to this category of consumer. Being a "first choice" employer for Gen Ys means that you will be able to harness their knowledge, insight and strengths along with those of their older colleagues.

Start by asking yourself these key questions:

1. What proportion of your workforce is Gen Y?
2. What is this figure likely to become over the next 3–5 years?
3. Now also ask the same questions about your customers and consumers.
4. Are you doing anything to specifically help your leaders lead your Gen Ys?
5. What are you doing to appeal to Gen Y customers and consumers?
6. What steps do you already have in place to ensure these young people don't leave?
7. Are you truly developing and harnessing young talent and providing a culture that fuels an innovative business?

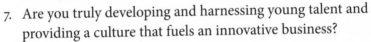

And, importantly:

8. What if you do nothing?

A solution or a problem?

Gen Y are only a manifestation of the massive technological change that is going on around us. We should not get fixated just on whether we, as employers or service providers, are adapting to meet their needs. It is more useful to see them as a catalyst for change, and to understand what opportunities they give us to learn about how we need to change. They can teach us about their world – the world of the digital native. Gen X and Boomers will always be immigrants in that world and will always, to some extent, have to "translate" their own "language" into the new languages.

There are those who are still treating Gen Y like a problem they need to manage. These people have not realized that Gen Y is one

144 indication that we are entering a new paradigm. And only by starting to understand that new paradigm will organizations be able to attract young employees and consumers now and in the future.

Rookie Buster

There are those who are still treating Gen Y like a problem they need to manage. These people have not realized that Gen Y is one indication that we are entering a new paradigm.

The irony is that the world that Gen Y have been brought up in is the world that has been created for them by Boomers and Gen X. Essentially, the older generations have shaped the way that Gen Y are. Until recently it was Boomers and Gen X who were inventing and designing the new technologies, and Boomers and Gen X are the parents of Gen Y. These same people are the ones I hear complaining about how difficult Gen Y is to manage, and the same people who ask whether Gen Y will change as a result of getting older and/or of economic realities. Of course they won't. We have created an environment that has resulted in a whole new set of behaviours, values and attitudes. The fundamental changes in the world cannot be unchanged, in the same way that Gen Y's conditioning and learning cannot be reversed – and nor should they be. We need them to be able to understand, respond to and keep on working at this changing paradigm.

Think about what different questions you need to ask in your organization to help you to get to grips with and respond to the changing paradigm. For example, if you are a charitable organization, you may well need to change your question from "How can we recruit new members and donors?" to "How can we channel and support the communities that support our cause so that they attract more people into those communities?" You can see how each of those questions might result in different solutions. The first might mean more content on their website and additional direct marketing campaigns. The latter 145 might mean having some of your employees blogging and twittering about things of interest to the communities in a way that enhances their experience of your organization and therefore increases their loyalty.

A new paradigm

As we have discussed so far in this chapter, it is important to be the sort of organization that Gen Y flock to work for. Having the best talent is essential in this fast-changing world.

Of course, the best organizations do have the best people. But nowadays the best companies realize that this is not enough. An excellent product, top class execution/delivery and a solid strategy are of course critical too.

But, because the paradigm is changing, a new mindset and way of working is necessary. The prevailing mindset was, and still is, a competitive one. Companies would guard their secrets and knowledge about the company. They would know who their competition was and keep an eye on them so that they could continue to stay at least one step ahead. Nowadays that is becoming a less and less sustainable model. The internet means that much more information and intelligence is available to the consumer. And companies can check out what their competitors are doing so much more easily. More and more companies are doing what Progressive Insurance do, which is to share their prices openly and share those of their competitors, even when their competitors are cheaper. The result is loyal customers who trust them.

The internet has made it possible for people

146   to collaborate openly. Linux, which is now widely used and recognized as a reliable operating system for business, started its life in 1991 when a man in Helsinki created a simple version of it and placed it on a bulletin board, inviting others to improve upon and develop it. They had access to it free of charge, and could use it provided that whatever changes they made they agreed to share. This way of working means that you attract a whole range of people, from all sorts of different disciplines and countries, to collaborate on a problem. You are no longer limited to the people you know or who work in your company. When The Economist Group set up a project to develop something new on the web a couple of years ago, the team who worked on it threw their challenge out to the wider community. They received hundreds of suggestions and ideas as well as creating a following, a buzz and an interest. Not all of it was positive – far from it. Some people criticized them for effectively asking for free help to develop what might become a profitable product. However, many more entered into the spirit of enquiry and collaboration.

Gen Y are used to this way of working. They use Wikipedia – a free website that is updated (without payment) by anyone who wants to update. They take this online encyclopedia for granted, whereas although the Boomers and Gen X may use and enjoy Wikipedia, they still compare it with the great big volumes that they had on their bookshelves at home when they were young. They think of it as that website that challenged *Encyclopaedia Britannica* and the successful encyclopedia publishing model in general.

The point is that if you don't understand well enough how the world is changing, or if you lose track of your market, you can literally find that your business collapses. This also happened to a certain degree in the stamp collecting field. Young people don't collect stamps to anywhere near the same degree as the older generations do. The stamp industry did not realize the scale of the issue early enough. It is crucially important to keep on learning about how the world is changing, about new models of doing business, about changing consumer behaviours and preferences and, of course, the impact of changing technologies.

Rookie Buster

If you don't understand well enough how the world is changing, or if you lose track of your market, you can literally find that your business collapses.

It is not a case of Gen Y setting out to destroy existing companies. It is a case of them experimenting and trying new and innovative ways of working and creating value through exploring different models and technologies.

From power to trust, competition to collaboration

Having great people is important, but it is not enough. A new competence is necessary to be able to thrive and survive in the changing world. That competence is collaboration. Some organizations can clearly be threatened and put out of business by this new openness and collaborative way of working. Encyclopedia publishers probably did not think of Wikipedia as a challenge to their business model at all to start with, let alone a serious challenge.

Rookie Buster

A new competence is necessary to be able to thrive and survive in the changing world. That competence is collaboration.

Some organizations are embracing collaboration as inevitable and to be welcomed. But it is a challenge because it threatens and calls into

148   question some ways of working and organizing that we have always taken for granted. It threatens the hierarchical model that is the most common model of organizing companies. And it challenges the power base of those at the top of the hierarchy.

Collaboration relies on people openly sharing their knowledge and insight. They have to trust that people are doing this and that they are being honest. This way of being is very familiar to Gen Y. They collaborate via the internet on all sorts of projects for school, for work and for their social interests. They are used to downloading content for free that others have posted, and they are used to sharing what they know. They use their network to rally people to help them on a whole range of projects – collaboration can be momentary and centred around a specific problem or question, or it can be much longer term, for example in the case of scientists working on a project together. Reciprocity and trust are central to collaborative relationships. Trust has always been important in life and business. And the best business relationships are founded on trust. The internet of course challenges us to achieve trust online and overcome all the fear and concerns that it produces.

Rookie Buster

Reciprocity and trust are central to collaborative relationships. Trust has always been important in life and business. And the best business relationships are founded on trust.

But of course there are mechanisms you can use to encourage and reward trust online. For example, the seller rating system on eBay means that consumers reward good service – they rate people on their reliability (did they send the goods when they said they would?) and honesty (did they accurately describe the items?). It is a self-managing system based on trust and social values. Yet when it was first set up sceptics said you could never trust the general public to deliver a good enough service and deliver on their promises. The sceptics have been proved wrong. It was a classic case of different thinking – thinking in a new paradigm. And traditional business people really struggled to see how it would work at the time. Now we pretty much all take it for granted.

Most management practices and organizational models are founded on the (often unconscious) assumption that you can't trust people, so you have to monitor them via a management hierarchy whose job it is to control those immediately below themselves. This way of structuring organization inhibits improvement and innovation, because you are limiting the number of people that each person has contact with.

Gen Y's world is not a hierarchical one. Theirs is a network of people with whom they interact for work or pleasure and often both. Even when you put them in a hierarchy (as most organizations do), it is as if they don't see it. A hierarchy does not of course have a physical presence. It is just a concept. Employees may be shown an organization chart that tells them their position (and relative importance and power). But it does not match with their natural way of working. Hence the cases of graduates emailing senior managers and not "going through" their own line management structure. It is not because they are being disrespectful; it is because they either couldn't see why they would need to do that, or it didn't occur to them that they might.

In my HR days I remember always telling staff with grievances or ideas that they should talk to their line manager first. That's just the way it was done. I never thought about why it had to be that way, let alone questioned that practice. Families used to be much more hierarchical than they are today, with the father at the top of the tree holding more power than the mother, who in turn held more power than the children. For Gen Y that has changed too – they are much more powerful and more often involved in and consulted about family decisions.

It is interesting and ironic that despite the fact that the family hierarchy has "loosened up" over recent years, that loosening-up process is much

150   harder and slower in the workplace. The hierarchical mindset is ingrained in the psyche and mindset of Boomers and Gen X. And so is the hierarchical model of organizations and work.

This presents a great challenge as well as a great opportunity, because Gen Y and the generations who follow them have experienced an empowered existence at home and expect to be consulted. Their way of working is a collaborative way. It is not that they are necessarily shunning the old ways of managing and organizing, it is just that some of these ways make no sense to them.

The Gen Y mindset will inevitably become the dominant mindset because it is in synch with the changing paradigm we have talked about. And as the young people of today become the managers of tomorrow, their way of working will inevitably be the dominant one.

Rookie Buster

The Gen Y mindset will inevitably become the dominant mindset.

Coach's notes

These are the most important points to remember from this book. Remember them, and you will avoid pitfalls and seize opportunities to make the most of Gen Y.

1. Gen Y are the way they are because of the very different context that they have grown up in. They are children of the digital age. They won't change and become like Gen X or Boomers. Their attitudes, values and ways of working are inherently different.

2. Be careful not to assume they are like the other generations – they are not. Making incorrect assumptions has wasted many organizations a lot of time and money (whether it is assumptions about how to attract Gen Y or assumptions about what would appeal to them as consumers). Always ask the question "What is important to the Gen Ys that I am trying to engage?"

3. Gen Ys love to learn, and are keen to learn from their older colleagues. Create an environment where they can learn from one another, and you will be able to release the knowledge, skills and unique strengths of all generations.

4. They will be in short supply as the global population ages. Good people will have a lot of choice about the type of work they do, whether they work for an organization and, if so, which organization they work for.

5. They are your consumers of the future. Understand them now and you will build the knowledge to retain them in the years ahead.

6. Don't rely on Gen X and Boomers to figure out what products, services and employment benefits will appeal to Gen Y. Instead, just *ask them*. It is impossible to second-guess what others would find appealing, particularly a group of people who have such different attitudes, values, habits and ways of working.

7. Involve Gen Y in strategy meetings, new product development meetings, meetings to devise graduate attraction strategies – basically, have them involved in any discussions that would benefit from real-life insight into this generation. It is surprising how many employees only see advertising campaigns or new products for the first time when they go public and consumers see them as well. This is a crazy waste of an invaluable resource.

8. See Gen Y as an opportunity – they can help you understand and respond to the changing digital world. If you see them as a challenge to be "managed", you will get left behind.

9. Constantly update your insight and understanding of your employees and consumers. We are talking about Gen Y in this book, but there is of course another generation coming after them, and they too will inevitably be different in some ways.

Go for it! A lot of what you have read about in this book is ways of working that have been known to be effective for a number of years. Gen Y embody these ways of working because of the conditions that they have grown up in. In the past, organizations could function without changing their ways. Soon they will no longer be able to do that without losing people, or business, or both. Delaying action will only mean that you end up having to make very large (and therefore very expensive) changes quickly. The good news is that you can start with some baby steps that will make a big difference. As long as you have good, deep insight into all generations, and you create an environment in which they thrive, you will be able to leverage all of their knowledge and unique strengths to respond to the changing environment. Good luck!

154

Notes

Appendix

Checklist: How Gen Y friendly is your organization?

Insight

1. Do you know what proportion of your workforce is Gen Y?
2. Do you know why they were attracted to come and work for you, and to what extent you have fulfilled your recruitment promise?
3. Do you understand what is really important to your employees and potential employees?
4. Do you regularly involve Gen Y in discussions about employment practices and listen to their views?
5. Do you have a good understanding of which of your practices and policies appeal most to which generation in your workforce?

Attraction and recruitment

6. Do you attract the calibre of Gen Y that you need?
7. Do you know what benefits appeal to your potential hires and why?
8. Do you know to what extent your communications media and messages appeal to Gen Y?

9. Do you hire people on their strengths as well as their competences?
10. Do you retain most of your Gen Ys, or do you over-hire expecting to lose some of them?
11. Do you recruit for the skills needed for the changing world of work, e.g. collaboration, listening and building trust-based relationships?
12. Do you hire the best people, whether or not they are graduates?
13. Have you changed your attraction and recruitment processes and methods to reflect the changing world of work and the nature of Gen Y as employees?

Engagement

14. Do you know what engages your Gen Ys?
15. If you have an engagement survey, does it reflect the values of all generations?
16. Do you teach your managers how to be engaging managers?
17. Do your communications strategy, content and style suit Gen Y's preferences?

Management

18. Do you have excellent mentors?
19. Do you teach your managers mentoring skills?
20. Do your managers understand Gen Y and how to manage them?

Organizational culture and communications

21. How collaborative is your organization culture?
22. Does your organization have a high-trust culture?
23. Do people feel comfortable challenging managers/senior managers?

24. Do managers/senior managers see Gen Y as a problem or an opportunity?
25. Do you have two-way communications channels?
26. Are your communications media, content and style Gen Y friendly?

Learning and development

27. Do you understand how Gen Y learn?
28. Do your development offerings and interventions reflect the preferences of all generations?
29. Do your trainers and facilitators understand Gen Y and how to design effective learning for them?

Team working

30. Do your employees understand different generational preferences?
31. Do you teach your people how to work effectively in cross-generational teams?

Career development

32. Do you understand what "career" means to your Gen Y employees and potential employees?
33. Do you regularly discuss their career progression and aspirations with your Gen Y employees?
34. Do you train your managers to help Gen Y to develop their careers and have excellent career development conversations?

158   Retention

35. Do you know why people stay?
36. Do you know why people leave?
37. Do your employees recommend you as an employer?

Using Gen Y's skills and unique strengths

38. Do you involve your Gen Y employees in developing your strategy and in designing and developing your products and services?

Top mistakes and top tips

Communicating with Gen Y

Top mistakes
- Power and status seen as more important than contribution.
- Communications one-way and written by Boomers and X-ers.
- Collaboration not encouraged.

Top tips
- Use up-to-date technologies for communication.
- Avoid spin.
- Have Gen Ys write your communications (style and content will be very different).
- Encourage participation.
- Organize networking activities.
- Create physical collaborative spaces.
- Create online collaborative spaces.

Managing Gen Y

Top mistakes
- Assuming they are like the other generations.
- Mistaking challenge for insubordination.
- Mistaking their ways of working for slacking/sloppiness.
- Monitoring not mentoring.
- Failing to give rationale for decisions.
- One-size-fits-all policies.

Top tips
- Create meaning and purpose as well as goals.
- Respect the knowledge and wisdom of both young and old.
- Show interest in individuals.
- Mentor not manage.
- Prefer trust over power.
- Support them, but let them get on with it.
- Manage the outcome, not the process.

Attracting and recruiting Gen Y

Top mistakes
- Not understanding what is really important to them.
- Not treating them as individuals.
- Using communication methods and styles that may not appeal.
- Ignoring key influencers.
- Relying too much on technology.
- Using "sifting" criteria that cut out a lot of good people.

Top tips
- Know their values as well as their interests.
- Talk to them in their language; avoid spin.
- Focus on their strengths.
- Use actions as well as words to show how good you are.
- Make sure your benefits have Gen Y appeal.

160 Developing Gen Y

Top mistakes
- Boomer/X-er style delivery.
- Failure to see learning as an ongoing process.
- Focusing too much on off-the-job.
- Providing development activities that don't appeal.
- Hiring trainers and consultants who don't understand Gen Y.
- Not realizing that learning is a source of stimulation and therefore engagement.

Top tips
- Understand them, their strengths and their interests.
- Make sure they know how to learn from and use the resources around them.
- Assign them to a (passionate) mentor.
- Constant feedback.
- Talk about what they are learning – a lot!
- E-learning solutions: on-demand, searchable, self-directed, YouTube-like.

Career development

Top mistakes
- "Career-ladder" mentality.
- Process above practicalities.
- Not helping people to understand their strengths and inherent talents.
- Treating people as a homogeneous group and not understanding what is important to individuals.
- A "secret" talent pool approach.

Top tips
- Understand what motivates each person.

- Make the most of their uniqueness instead of squeezing into an
  "all-rounder" box.
- "Teach" them how to learn – a crucial career skill.
- Emphasize continuous learning.
- Engage managers and mentors in ongoing support.
- Work with them to set up a peer network.

Cross-generational teamworking

Top mistakes
- Not understanding the teamworking styles and preferences of different generations.
- Running teams in a hierarchical way that doesn't value the contribution of each member.
- Not understanding the strengths and unique contribution of each person in the team.
- Forcing each team member to work in the same way without taking account of their individual style and preferences.

Top tips
- Teach teams how to work well together.
- Help them understand generational differences.
- Focus on the team process and the individuals as well as the task.

Index